TASTY

DESSERT

all the sweet you can eat

CLARKSON POTTER/PUBLISHERS
New York

CONTENTS

INTRODUCTION

If you've ever gone to town on a pint of ice cream after a long, hard day, you understand the restorative power of a good dessert. (It's called self-care, okay??) But while we at Tasty love a good store-bought treat as much as anyone—hey, we're not made of stone-ground flour!—we think a homemade dessert is truly in a class of its own. Turning your pantry basics into a mouthwatering (and, of course, Instagram-ready) sweet treat is part science, part art, and all Tasty.

Even the simplest baked treat can transform the most unexceptional event into an absolute occasion. Don't believe us? We dare you to bring a plate of Crème Brûlée Cookies to your most boring meeting this week and see what happens. And if a dessert can raise the game on the everyday, imagine what it can do for those *really* special moments! Look, we could write volumes of love poetry to veggies, but there's a reason we cap off birthdays and weddings with cake and not a roasted beet salad. Desserts are just so—forgive us—*extra*.

Because desserts take pretty much everything to the next level, it's only fitting that you level up your baking skills. Which is exactly where we come in! We'll take you from batter beginner to master baker before you can say *pâte à choux*. Not a newbie? Not a problem! We've got tips, tricks, updates, and spins to help you pastry vets *rise* to any occasion. Whether you're yearning for a spiffy take on a nostalgic favorite (helloooooo No-Bake 16-Layer S'Mores Cake) or want to experiment with new flavors (we see you, Matcha Macarons), we've got your *bake*.

We're all about the showstopping creations you can make with the ingredients you probably already have in your kitchen (get ready to meet Checkerboard Cake and Ice Cream Churro Bowls). We're on team chewy AND team crispy. We're here for chocolate and for fruit (sometimes both at once). But mostly, we're here for delicious. So if you're ready for miniaturized, stuffed, layered, striped, twisted, frosted, and meringued, you're ready for this book.

Just remember this: While the best part of dessert may be sharing, always save a serving for yourself.

ready, steady, bake!

Baking may be a science, but deciding *what* to bake is more of an art. Whether you're inspired by the weather, your horoscope, or something you just saw on Instagram, there's no denying that there's nothing practical about a craving. It's a feeling—an instinct! And more than any other element of a dessert, it's texture that determines what you're in the mood for: silky-creamy when you need a big hug, crunchy-crackly when you're feeling sassy. We organized the chapters so that when you've had a *day* and your body's screaming "CHOCOLATE!," you can beeline to "Dense & Fudgy" for a brownie so cocoa-packed it could hold up a skyscraper. But when you've got some pep in your step and need fresh and juicy, you can turn to "Juicy & Fruity" and pick up all the blueberries you can carry for a summer pie extravaganza.

We've put a Beyoncé-level iconic recipe at the beginning of each chapter—so for "Creamy Dreamy," that's cheesecake, and for "Crunchy, Crackly, Crispy," that's the compulsively crunchable Honeycomb Toffee—and then added tons of ideas for how to switch up the ways to make it (and/or eat it) to fit your own personal style. So not *just* toffee, but toffee dipped into melted chocolate for crunchy bark. And not *just* cheesecake but cheesecake topped with cookie butter or August peaches. Take one kind of frosting and make it into eight kinds. Are you picking up what we're putting down?

Within every chapter we've got a wide range of recipes, from soon-to-be viral hits (like the Strawberry Rose Crepe Cake) to weeknight-friendly, ready-in-30 faves (what monster would turn down a Soft and Chewy Snickerdoodle?) you could make with your eyes closed (but, um, don't try that). For every all-day affair that puts your pastry chops to work, there's a no-bake, mostly hands-off indulgence with a payoff so much greater than your investment (the hardest part of the Rocky Road Ice Cream Cake? Waiting for it to freeze!). And don't think we forgot gluten-free (shout-out to the Flourless Chocolate Torte) and vegan-friendly (the Dairy-Free Carrot Cake doesn't miss the butter) desserts, too—no matter who you're baking for, they'll come away very happy.

INGREDIENTS

If bakers are magicians (and let's be clear, they are), ingredients are the tools to their tricks. With the right sequence, combination, and environment, ho-hum kitchen staples—eggs, flour, butter, sugar—can transform into soft, fluffy cakes or shatteringly crisp cookies. But you've got to know which to use and when the differences actually matter. Here's the 411:

Dry Ingredients

FLOUR: We bakers salute **all-purpose flour**, aka AP flour (street name: white flour). Common and versatile, it's in nearly every supermarket. You can use bleached or unbleached, enriched or not, whatever your preference dictates. Once you move beyond all-purpose, the options abound:

- **Cake flour** has a lower protein content, which makes for softer baked goods with a lighter crumb and a finer texture. If you don't want to buy it, replace 2 tablespoons of every cup of AP flour with cornstarch.

- **Pastry flour** has a protein level in between AP flour and cake flour.

- **Bread flour** has more protein than AP to encourage the gluten development that allows yeasted loaves to rise high and maintain their structure.

- **Self-rising flour** already has leaveners (hence the name), as well as salt. To make your own, add ¼ teaspoon salt and 1¼ teaspoons baking powder to every cup of AP flour.

- **Whole-wheat flour** includes the bran and germ in the flour. This gives your goods a heartier, nuttier flavor and a darker color. Whole-wheat flour makes for denser baked goods and, unless a recipe is specifically written for 100% whole-wheat flour, works best when combined with white flour.

- And finally, when we say **gluten-free flour,** we're talking store-bought mixes—like Cup4Cup or Bob's Red Mill—that can be substituted for AP.

NUT FLOURS: Any nut you can think of can be ground into a super flavorful flour (sometimes called "meal"). Almond meal, for one, can be used to make a gluten-free chocolate cake or pristine macarons, but it can also be swapped in for a small portion of flour in nearly any cake recipe to lend an extra-tender texture. Since nut flours are so fatty, they're prone to spoilage; store them in the freezer near your alternative flours to extend their lives.

CORNMEAL: At its most basic, cornmeal is dried and ground corn that can range from fine to coarse. When you see "stone-ground" cornmeal, that means that some of the bran and germ is included (in most commercial production, it's discarded), which means the meal will stay a bit crunchy and gritty after it's baked. Corn flour is just very finely ground cornmeal, and polenta, as you'll see it at the supermarket, is basically medium-ground cornmeal that's appropriate for making the Italian dish of the same name.

SALT: Batman has Robin, good has evil, Pinky has The Brain, and sugar has salt. Without it, your baked goods will taste flat and muted. Use kosher salt for all your basic baking. But for gilding your gooiest chocolate chip cookie, turn to a fancy garnishing salt like fleur de sel, a moist French sea salt, or a flaky sea salt like Maldon salt, which has crystals the size of small diamonds.

CORNSTARCH: Cornstarch thickens puddings, pie fillings, frozen desserts, pastry creams, and jams. To stop it from clumping up, whisk it with a small portion of the recipe's total sugar and the total liquid before adding it.

OATS: Unless otherwise noted, bake with old-fashioned rolled oats, but quick-cooking oats won't ruin your muffins or loaf cakes. In general, stay away from baking with instant oats, which will disappear into your batter, and steel-cut oats, which will forever remain like gerbil pellets.

NUTS: Because they can go rancid (meaning: sour, bitter, smelly, altogether gross) rather quickly, store them in jars or bags in the refrigerator or freezer. To bring out their full flavor (and make them so much more delicious to snack on), toast nuts on a parchment-lined sheet tray in a 350°F oven for 5 to 10 minutes, until irresistibly fragrant and a shade or two darker.

Fats

BUTTER: Most baking recipes call for unsalted butter, which puts you in total control of the saltiness of the finished product. You can store butter in the freezer for months, but be sure to allow plenty of time for it to sit out and get to the right temperature before you start baking.

VEGETABLE SHORTENING: A solid fat made from vegetable oils, it creates flaky pie crusts and sky-high biscuits. It also inhibits gluten production, which makes for softer, more tender baked goods.

COCONUT OIL: Solid at room temperature, it makes for darn-good vegan baked goods without the need for vegetable-based butter substitutes. Refined coconut oil has a more neutral taste than virgin coconut oil, which can smell distinctly coconutty. You can liquify coconut oil by placing it in a hot water bath or warming it in the microwave or on the stovetop.

OIL: When a recipe in this book calls for a neutral oil, use a vegetable oil like canola, safflower, or sunflower. When you want the flavor of the oil to

shine, use olive oil. All oils are light and temperature sensitive, so store them in a cool, dry place and take a good whiff before use to ensure they haven't gone rancid.

Sugars & Sweeteners

GRANULATED SUGAR: When a recipe here calls for "sugar," it's referring to the white granular stuff, refined from sugarcane, that makes the medicine go down. Organic sugar is a vegan-friendly alternative, though the grain can be a bit coarser. Throw it in the food processor to make smaller granules that'll melt at the same rate as the regular stuff.

CONFECTIONERS' SUGAR: Also known as powdered or icing sugar, it's light, clumpy, and bound to get all over your counters and clothing. Before you use it, sift it to eliminate most lumps.

BROWN SUGAR: This is simple white sugar with molasses added back for color and flavor (dark has more, light brown has less). Avoid the problem of rock-hard brown sugar by storing it in an airtight container in your pantry.

RAW SUGARS: Muscovado, demerara, and turbinado sugars are also made from sugarcane, but they're less processed than white sugar, so they stay like sparkly crystals on the surface of pies, scones, and loaf cakes. Crunch, crunch.

HONEY: Honeys vary tremendously in flavor and texture, depending on the flower source; some are delicate and floral, others are bold and spicy. If you're unsure of the strength of the honey, use its color as a rough guide: lighter honeys, like orange blossom and clover, have a milder flavor, whereas the darker ones, like chestnut and buckwheat, are more powerful.

MAPLE SYRUP: If you're having trouble navigating the maple syrups at the store, just remember: The darker the syrup, the bolder the flavor. Golden-looking syrups, which taste subtle and mild, are best drizzled on fruit or waffles, while the mid-range, amber-hued stuff lends that classic maple flavor to pies, loaves, and glazes. Save the darkest shades, harvested later in the season, for when you want a slam of maple intensity in gingerbread cookies and spice cakes.

MOLASSES: Mild and sweet light molasses can generally be swapped freely for the thicker, more robust dark molasses, depending on your taste preference. But don't use blackstrap molasses—the least sweet and the most bitter—unless a recipe calls for it. Look for molasses labeled "unsulfured," as it is free of the preservative sodium dioxide and is made from mature, naturally ripened sugarcane.

CORN SYRUP: This stuff helps prevent crystallization in candy and frozen desserts; it keeps baked goods from drying out, and it adds gloss, smoothness, and neutral sweetness to sauces, fillings, and frostings. Don't substitute dark corn syrup when light is called for—it has a stronger flavor and different appearance.

Leaveners

BAKING POWDER: Baking powder acts twice to give your biscuits, cakes, and quick breads loft and lift: first when it's mixed with liquid ingredients, and again when it interacts with the heat from the oven.

BAKING SODA: While baking powder can operate on its own, baking soda needs help activating from an acidic ingredient, like buttermilk, yogurt, or even coffee or canned pumpkin. Baking soda almost never expires, but the box you keep in your fridge to absorb the smells from take-out food—don't use that one in your cake.

YEAST: For the majority of baking recipes, stick to active dry yeast—the kind that comes in those neat three-packs—not instant yeast. Store yeast in an airtight container in the refrigerator or freezer, where it will last for up to a year.

Dairy & Eggs

MILK: We beg you: Don't substitute anemic skim milk when full-bodied whole milk is called for. The recipe might work, but it won't reach its full potential! While milk is perishable, it's often processed into shelf-stable forms that you can keep on hand for anytime baking. Evaporated milk is a concentrated canned milk with about 60 percent of the water removed; sweetened condensed milk is a close cousin, only the addition of sugar makes it syrupy and caramelized; and milk powder has zero moisture, meaning it can make ice cream creamier, puddings richer, and bread more golden-brown.

NONDAIRY MILKS: Different types vary in fat content and flavor, so only use these where milk doesn't play a large role in the recipe (soy milk might be fine for a loaf cake, for example, but don't try to make it into pastry cream).

COCONUT MILK: Unless otherwise instructed, buy cans of unsweetened coconut milk and save the sweetened stuff for piña coladas. Shake the can before you open it in order to recombine the thick coconut cream with the watery liquid below.

BUTTERMILK: Tangy and acidic, it makes muffins, pancakes, quick breads, scones, and biscuits tender-er. But if you don't have buttermilk, you can MacGyver some. For each cup of buttermilk you need, pour a scant cup of whole milk, then add a spoonful of white vinegar or lemon juice until you reach your volume goal. Mix it well, then let it sit for 5 to 10 minutes.

YOGURT: Most recipes will specify whether yogurt should be the plain variety or the thick and creamy Greek-style. If you only have Greek yogurt handy, you can replace a tablespoon or two of the total quantity with water or milk to make a thinner mixture that will serve you just as well. Whatever you do, use full-fat yogurt and don't swap in flavored, sweetened, or fruity versions.

CREAM: Don't stress too much about the labels: You can use heavy cream, whipping cream, or heavy whipping cream—it's all good. Cream aerates best when it's cold, and you can also chill your whisk and bowl for extra efficiency. And there's no need to buy half-and-half, which is equal parts milk and light cream: Simply mix the two liquids together in equal proportion, *et voilà*.

SOUR CREAM: Made from cultured cream, sour cream is naturally thick, rich, and tangy. It's a delight in cheesecake, coffee cake, and biscuits.

CRÈME FRAÎCHE: Crème fraîche is similar to sour cream, only it's even richer and fattier, with no added stabilizers. It doesn't curdle when warmed, and it can be whipped with heavy cream into a billowy topping for pies, poached fruit, and cobblers. To make it yourself, mix together 1 cup of cream and 2 tablespoons of buttermilk, cover the container, and let it sit at room temperature until thick and luscious, 12 to 24 hours. Look at you go!

CREAM CHEESE: For baking, buy cream cheese in blocks rather than tubs. It'll be easier to measure (the measurements are marked on the package, just like a stick of butter) and chop into chunks. When your cream cheese needs to be at room temp, don't rush it.

EGGS: Unless a recipe instructs you otherwise, use large eggs. If you're tasked with separating the whites from the yolks, know that it's easiest to work with cold eggs. But since it's better to whip whites at room temperature, separate your eggs earlier in the process and let the egg whites hang out until you're ready for them.

Chocolate

CHOCOLATE BARS: Bittersweet and semisweet can be used interchangeably, though semisweet is generally a teensy bit sweeter. You'll want to look at the cocoa percentage on the packaging (a higher percentage indicates a stronger, less sweet chocolate) and do some taste-testing, since you should bake with what you like to eat. Creamy, mild milk chocolate includes more sugar and milk solids. And then there's white chocolate: It contains no cocoa solids and is made instead with cocoa butter, milk solids, sugar, and an emulsifier that binds it all together. Take caution: White chocolate melts faster than the others, so keep a close watch.

CHOCOLATE CHIPS: Reserve them for places where you want chocolate pieces to stay intact (cookies, blondies, muffins). They have too many stabilizers to make silky smooth ganache.

COCOA POWDER: There are two camps of cocoa powder. Natural cocoa powder is untreated, which makes it sharp, strong, and complex, whereas Dutch-processed cocoa is washed with an alkaline solution, which neutralizes the acid and results in a mellower flavor and a richer color. Use your powder of preference in any recipe that doesn't get leavened (hot cocoa, fudge sauce, frostings). But when baking powder or soda is in the mix, stick with whatever's instructed.

Flavors, Extracts & Other Goodies

EXTRACTS: In addition to the classic vanilla, you can find lemon, almond, peppermint, cinnamon, and even banana extracts. Oh, baby! Add them little by little, incorporating by the drop rather than the teaspoonful.

COFFEE: In addition to waking you up in the morning, coffee makes chocolate taste, well, more chocolatey. Some recipes will call for dry instant espresso powder, while others call for strongly brewed coffee, in which case you can make the instant espresso and mix it in.

GELATIN: Gelatin turns liquid into jiggly, jelly solids (think: mousses, gummies, panna cottas, and marshmallows) and comes in two forms. To use powdered gelatin, sprinkle it over the specified amount of cold water or liquid and wait for it to turn spongy, about 5 minutes. Then microwave it for 15 seconds, and stir until liquified. Soak gelatin sheets (also called leaf gelatin) in a large amount of cold water for 5 to 10 minutes, then gently wring them out. Either add them to warm liquid, as explained in the recipe, or—if mixing into cold liquid—melt them very slowly in the microwave or a saucepan first.

DRIED FRUIT: These are always available, no matter the season, but don't subject your desserts to hard, shriveled dried fruit. To re-plump, pour boiling-hot water (you could also use alcohol, juice, or—for something sharp—vinegar) over the fruit and let stand for a few minutes. Drain and pat dry before using.

NUT BUTTERS: Natural and homemade nut butters taste great, but they tend to be grainier, with a layer of oil that's hard to recombine with the solids. Unless otherwise specified, use an old-fashioned peanut butter (you know, like Skippy or Jif brands) for cakes, cookies, and loaves.

TAHINI: A savory, nutty sauce made from ground sesame seeds, tahini is kind of like nut butter, but different. It can be mixed into buttercream, folded into cake batters, subbed in for peanut butter in cookie dough, or even creamed into frangipane. If you notice that oil has risen to the top of the jar and left a thick, pasty layer below, take care to do some good mixing before you start baking (you might have to break out the food processor).

PUFF PASTRY: Perfect for making tarts, palmiers, danishes, and pastries that look like they came straight from a bakery. Thaw it for 20 to 30 minutes at room temp (watch closely—it can go sticky and soft in an instant) or overnight in the refrigerator before rolling it out on a lightly floured surface. Shape it as you want, then watch it grow into a million layers in the oven. Keep any extra pieces covered with a damp paper towel to prevent them from drying out.

SPICES: When sweater weather hits, cinnamon, ginger, nutmeg, cloves, allspice, and black pepper come out to play in gingerbread, spice cakes, and pies of all kinds. Buy them often and in small amounts, and take a whiff before using— if your spice has lost its fragrance and vibrancy, it's time to replace it.

NONSTICK COOKING SPRAY: Use an unflavored canola-oil-based spray to prep pans that are a pain to butter or oil evenly (bundts, muffin tins, waffle irons) and to help parchment paper stick to pans when lining them.

COCONUT: Choose between the dramatic and showy flakes or the confetti-like shreds, which come sweetened or unsweetened. Both are toastier, crispier, and altogether more delicious after a stint in the oven, unless the recipe specifies untoasted.

EQUIPMENT

You know how we said ingredients are like magical spells? Well, that makes the equipment the magic wand. Without the right tools, the ingredients just can't do their thing. Some of these are as essential as a heartbeat, while others are a little more, shall we say, aspirational. We'll start with the critical players and move down the line to the extra-credit accessories.

Utensils & Other Small Helpers

SPATULAS: A flexible rubber or silicone spatula is great for nudging batter from the bowl to your pan or gently folding together fragile ingredients. For mesmerizing buttercream swoops on a cake's surface, use an offset spatula, either big or little, to act like a third hand.

WOODEN SPOON: This good old-fashioned guy is not as gentle or spry as a spatula, but it succeeds in smashing together butter and sugar (when you're creaming without the help of a machine), mixing eggs into cream puff dough, and all sorts of other tasks where a delicate hand is not necessary.

WHISKS: There are lots of specialty whisks out there (French, flat, spiral, coil, cage), each of which has its pluses and minuses. But if you're going to have just one kind, go for the widely available and versatile balloon whisk, which is shaped like a teardrop. It'll bring cream to soft peaks and eliminate lumps in batters, no problemo. We also like to have a smaller whisk on hand for the littler jobs.

MICROPLANE OR OTHER FINE GRATER: Necessary for getting ultra-fine shreds of citrus zest or snowy gratings of fresh nutmeg.

ROLLING PIN: Stick with the French-style (a solid wooden cylinder, kind of like a baseball bat) instead of the ball-bearing American-style (a cylinder that rolls around a shaft, with a handle on each end), as it gives you greater control. If you're in a pinch, a bottle of wine works great, too.

BOX GRATER: A love of carrot cake is reason enough to make room in your kitchen for a simple metal box grater with different perforations on each side. But it also shreds apples and turns chocolate bars into fancy shavings that can be piled on top of mud pie or ice cream.

TIMER: Even if you have impeccable natural timing skills, you still don't want to leave the fate of your cake up to chance. If you don't have a separate timing device, use your phone. It's a good idea to check the oven five to ten minutes *before* the minimum suggested baking time for extra insurance.

OVEN MITTS: This sounds like an obvious addition to any kitchen—but remember that time you had to use a sweatshirt to shimmy the pie out of the oven? Get a pair of thick, protective mitts to protect your most valuable baking tool (no, not your manicure—your hands!). If necessary, you can always use a dry dish towel or two.

MEASURING CUPS AND SPOONS: Use liquid ones (the glass guys with spouts) for, um, duh, liquid ingredients and dry ones (graduated metal or plastic sets) for dry ingredients, period.

MIXING BOWLS: A nesting set will save you both space and moolah. Make sure at least some are microwave-safe and/or heatproof, meaning they won't shatter if you pour in a hot syrup or nestle them above a pot of simmering water. Bonus points for bowls with spouts, which make transferring sloshy mixtures less messy.

COOLING RACKS: These are the home for your baked goods while you stand by in anticipation, counting down the minutes until the first bite. Racks not only protect your counters from hot pans, but they also allow air to circulate underneath for even cooling. But read the recipe carefully: Some baked goods need to rest in the pan until they're ready to be flipped out, while others get transferred to cooling racks right away, so that they don't continue to bake on a hot sheet.

FINE-MESH SIEVES: If you have a large fine-mesh sieve, you can simply add your dry ingredients and shake, shake, shake. It'll also come to the rescue for straining custards, caramels, ice cream bases, and puddings. Buy a set of three sizes. You'll reach for the smaller ones when you need to strain lemon juice, dust a cake with powdered sugar, or make yourself a celebratory cocktail.

Materials

PARCHMENT PAPER: Let parchment paper be your baking hero—let it take away your pain. Heatproof, nonstick, and reusable (for up to two or three non-messy bakes), it'll ensure that your cake doesn't stick to the pan and that your cookies don't get too dark or wide on the baking sheet.

SILICONE BAKING MATS: For an eco-friendly alternative to parchment sheets, invest in oven-, microwave-, and dishwasher-safe silicone baking sheets. They come in a variety of shapes and sizes, and some even have stencils to help you roll out your dough to the right size or pipe perfect macarons.

SAUCEPANS: We bakers may seem like oven-worshippers, but some sweets—caramel, toffee, beignets—require the stove. You'll want a big, heavy-bottomed pot for frying and candy-making, plus a wee pot for browning butter, warming milk, or melting ganache.

BAKING SHEETS: Rimmed baking sheets are the most versatile, able to contain any ingredients that could ooze (like roasted fruit) or scatter (like toasted nuts). If the sides are high enough, you'll be able to use a rimmed baking sheet to bake crowd-feeding sheet cakes, bar cookies, and slab pies. Half-sheet pans (18 by 13 inches) are the standard; look for heavy-duty aluminum sheets and avoid dark-colored ones that will make your goods brown faster than you want 'em to.

BUNDT PAN: With curves in all the right places, bundt cakes always look a little dressed up, even when you don't glaze them. Most recipes are written for 10- or 12-cup pans. Nonstick is the best option for all of those nooks and crannies—but you'll still want to butter and flour the pan to ensure no stubborn stickiness. Look for one with a cool design if you want to be extra impressive.

TUBE PANS: With their straight sides and, often, removable bottoms, these are intended for delicate cakes, like angel food and chiffon, that rely on the shape for structure. They sometimes have little arms poking out of the top to lift the pan off the counter as it cools upside down.

LOAF PAN: Essential for b-a-n-a-n-a bread and all sorts of other delicious loaves and quick breads and yeasted pull-apart beauties. A 9 by 5-inch loaf pan that's 3 inches tall will work for most recipes. Look for light-colored (and preferably nonstick) metal for even baking and easy unmolding.

MUFFIN TIN: You can use a 12-cup nonstick muffin tin for cupcakes, mini pies or tarts, crispy rice cups, and—obvs—muffins. Like all good things, they come in mini, too!

CAKE PANS: You want pans that are heavy duty and light in color, so that the outside doesn't get too dark before the inside cooks through. In terms of sizes, you're in tip-top shape if you have two 8-inch and 9-inch round pans; a 9-inch springform pan (for cheesecakes, tortes, and any cakes you'll want to unmold but can't flip out); an 8-inch square pan; and a 9 by 13-inch pan.

TART PAN WITH REMOVABLE BOTTOM: You'll need one of these to make elegant tarts with pristine fluted edges (the 9½-inch size should do the trick). But if you just need to make a fruit tart and don't want to take the pan plunge, you can use a springform pan in its place (though the results won't be quite as neat).

PIE PLATES: Glass pie dishes can be useful for beginners (they cook fillings evenly and allow you to examine the color of the crust as it bakes), but metal pans conduct heat more efficiently, yielding a crispier bottom crust. A deep-dish pie plate will have higher sides, accommodating more recipes (and more apple filling). Pro tip: If you're baking a pie that might bubble over, bake it on a parchment-lined sheet tray to avoid an oven mess.

PIE WEIGHTS: When you want to bake a pie crust without a filling, you'll need pie weights. Pie weights literally weigh down the dough in its tin so it keeps its shape while baking; the baked pie crust can then be filled with all sorts of no-bake fillings, like puddings, gelatin-based chiffon, or fruit jam and preserves. Pie weights are sold in baking stores and online as ceramic or metal beads that can be used over and over, but you can also simply use dried beans or rice (just make sure to never try to cook with them afterward!). To use them, line your raw pie dough with a sheet of parchment paper and fill the entire volume of the dish with your weights. Once you're done baking with the weights, remove them from the pie tin by using the parchment paper as handles, let them cool down completely, then store them in a resealable container. If using rice or beans, as long as you keep them dry, they'll keep indefinitely.

Machines

STAND MIXER: Humans have baked successfully without stand mixers for eons—if you don't have one, you'll do just fine with a wooden spoon and a bit of arm strength. But we won't lie: They're lifesavers when it comes to baking tasks that take a lot of horsepower, like whipping egg whites to stiff, glossy peaks or kneading dough for 10 minutes straight. For a fraction of the price, a handheld electric mixer can do a good portion of what a stand mixer can (and is all you'll need to bake your way through this book).

FOOD PROCESSOR: Sometimes we confuse our food processor for our best friend. Oops. It chops nuts, purees jams, grinds freeze-dried fruit, and shreds carrots—it can even whip cream and knead dough! Food processors also come in handy for making tender, flaky baked goods—like pie crust, scones, biscuits, and shortbread—because they incorporate butter quickly without overworking the dough.

WHAT GREAT BAKERS KNOW

What makes one baker better than another? It's nothing supernatural. Nope, it's mostly paying attention to the little details that end up making a big difference. Here's what to do so your sweet adventures fly, not flop.

Read the recipe all the way through before you start.

We know you're so ready to get going, but take a sec to read through *all* of the directions—and we mean all of them. You'll see if you need any special equipment, if you should prep any ingredients ahead of time, or if there's a critical part of the recipe that has to happen quickly. If that's the case, you'll want to measure out the key players (and set up any equipment) before you get the ball rolling.

Take the temperature.

When it comes to baking, your ingredients need to be at the right temperature (we're talking room temp egg whites, or cold butter, or soft cream cheese) in order to reach the proper consistency. And your oven temperature is just as important: If it's too hot, the outside of your cake might dry out before it's cooked through; if it's too cold, your pie crust might leak butter instead of becoming crisp and flaky. Wait patiently for the oven to come up to temperature and get a thermometer so you can check its work. If a recipe tells you to bake on the bottom, middle, or top rack, listen.

Don't substitute recklessly.

You know that joke where an online commenter substitutes either Splenda or cottage cheese for every ingredient in a recipe and then wonders what went wrong? Don't be that person. When an ingredient isn't going to mess with the ecosystem of the baked good (let's say you want to swap out cinnamon for cardamom, or ¼ cup of crème fraîche for sour cream), you can make a change. But when you're messing with the ratio of wet to dry ingredients, or the chemical reactions, or the gluten levels, you do so at your own risk.

Set a timer—and check often!

Baking is not a "set it and forget it" situation. Stay close to your kitchen and ready your nose for smells of doneness. We recommend checking halfway through the suggested bake time. You can see if anything's gone wrong (maybe your pie is about to bubble over and you want to put a sheet pan below it) or if you need to rotate the pan or trays. Then set another timer to go off five minutes before the time listed in the recipe—you can always add more time to soft cookies but you can't reverse the burnt ones.

Let the baked goods cool as instructed—even if it's hard.

It can be so, so mind-blowingly difficult to wait for a cake to cool (and don't get us started on cheesecakes that need to chill completely, or ice cream that needs to freeze), but please take that last step of the recipe just as seriously as the middle ones. You risk compromising all of your hard work if you frost a cake while it's too warm or slice into a pie straight out of the oven. Distract yourself with a TV show or Pokémon Go if it helps you to endure the wait.

DENSE & FUDGY

one brownie 100 ways

These brownies are chocolatey and a little gooey when you take them out of the oven. If you have the faith (and patience) to let them cool completely, you'll avoid molten chocolate and be rewarded with truffle-like bars. For those of you who like a slightly cakier brownie with some chew (we won't judge), go for those perimeter pieces. The rest of us will fight for the middle.

If you need some crunch, creaminess, or pop, we've got a hundred ideas for doodads and embellishments to fold into the batter at the very last moment.

1¼ cups (2½ sticks) **unsalted butter**, plus more, at room temperature, for greasing

8 ounces **semisweet** or **bittersweet chocolate** (60 to 70% cacao), coarsely chopped

¾ cup **unsweetened Dutch-processed cocoa powder**

1 tablespoon **espresso powder**

2 cups **granulated sugar**

½ cup packed **dark brown sugar**

2 teaspoons **kosher salt**

2 teaspoons **vanilla extract**

6 large **eggs**

1 cup **all-purpose flour**

1   Preheat the oven to 350°F. Grease a 9 by 13-inch dark metal baking pan with butter, then line it with parchment paper, leaving 1 inch of overhang on all sides, and grease the parchment.

2   In a heatproof liquid measuring cup, combine the chopped chocolate, ¼ cup of the cocoa powder, and the espresso powder.

3   Bring the butter to a boil in a small saucepan over medium heat. Pour the hot butter over the chocolate mixture and let sit for 2 minutes, undisturbed, then whisk until smooth.

4   Combine the granulated sugar, brown sugar, salt, vanilla, and eggs in a large bowl. Using a handheld mixer, beat on high speed until light and fluffy, about 10 minutes. The texture will be similar to that of pancake batter.

5   With the mixer running, pour in the chocolate mixture and beat until smooth. Sift the remaining ½ cup cocoa powder and the flour into the batter and use a rubber spatula to gently fold them in until just combined.

6   Pour the batter into the prepared pan and smooth out the top with the spatula. Bake until lightly puffed on top, about 20 minutes. Remove the baking pan from the oven (keep the oven on) and lightly tap the pan against a flat surface once or twice until the brownies deflate slightly.

7   Return the pan to the oven and bake until a wooden skewer inserted halfway between the center and the sides comes out with just a few crumbs attached, about 20 minutes more. The center of the brownies will seem underbaked, but the brownies will continue to set as they cool. Transfer the baking pan to a wire rack and let the brownies cool completely in the pan, about 2 hours.

8   Using the parchment paper as handles, lift the cooled brownies out of the pan and set them on a cutting board. Cut into 24 bars and serve or store in an airtight container at room temperature for up to 1 week.

MIX-INS

After folding in the flour and cocoa powder at the end of Step 5, stir in 1 cup of mix-ins from the first section; 2 tablespoons of mix-ins from the second section; or, after the batter is smoothed in the pan, swirl ½ cup of mix-ins from the third section on top, before baking.

1 cup

Chopped dark chocolate

Chopped walnuts

Chopped pecans

Chopped peanuts

Chopped almonds

Chopped pistachios

Chopped macadamias

Chopped hazelnuts

M&M's

Oreos, chopped

Pretzels, chopped

Potato chips, lightly crushed

Peanut butter cups, chopped

Mini marshmallows

Butterscotch chips

White chocolate chips

Milk chocolate chips

Coconut flakes

Dried cherries

Dried apricots, chopped

Dried pineapple, chopped

Dried cranberries

Raisins

Soft caramel candies

Yogurt chips

Cookie dough, chopped into ½-inch pieces

Gummy bears

Sprinkles

Swedish Fish, chopped

Toffee chips

Rice Krispies

Cinnamon Toast Crunch

Fruity Pebbles

Granola

Graham crackers, chopped

Butterfinger candy bars, chopped

Cap'n Crunch

Pepitas (pumpkin seeds)

Sunflower seeds

Kit Kats, chopped

Candied orange peel, chopped

Animal crackers

Waffle cones, chopped

Truffles, halved

Licorice, chopped

Snickers, chopped

Halva, chopped

Baklava, chopped

Malt balls, chopped

Andes mints, chopped

Mochi, chopped

Caramel corn

Cacao nibs

Chocolate-covered espresso beans

Banana bread, cubed

Rock candy

Bananas, thinly sliced

Guava paste, chopped

Trail mix

Pocky sticks, chopped

Sesame sticks

Dates, chopped

Dried figs, chopped

Peppermints/candy canes, chopped

Stroopwafels, chopped

Pirouline cookies, chopped

Shortbread cookies, chopped

Ritz crackers, chopped

Fresh blueberries

Fresh cherries

Candied cherries

Nonpareils

Red Hots candies

Peppermint Patties, chopped

Pomegranate seeds

Biscotti cookies, chopped

Doughnut holes, chopped

Ladyfingers, chopped

Cooked bacon, chopped

Vanilla wafers, chopped

Candy corn

2 tablespoons

Sesame seeds

Candied ginger, finely chopped

Chia seeds

Freshly grated orange zest

Flaky sea salt

Cayenne pepper

Matcha powder

Dried lavender

½ cup

Cream cheese

Nutella

Cookie butter

Raspberry jam

Orange marmalade

Blueberry jam

Marshmallow Fluff

Tahini

Peanut butter

Dulce de leche

Almond butter

Canned pumpkin purée

SPRINKLES

BANANA BREAD

BROWNIES

CANDIED GINGER

COOKIE BUTTER

SWEDISH FISH

DULCE DE LECHE

COOKIE DOUGH

WHITE CHOCOLATE
CHIPS

CANDIED CHERRIES

RITZ CRACKERS

DOUBLE CHOCOLATE
MOUSSE TART

If you think that mousse is so spoonably airy that it must be finicky, fear not. Ours is made with just two ingredients—chocolate chips and whipped cream—that get folded together before setting in the fridge into a spongy custard you can sink your spoon into, with an intense chocolatey flavor that defies its cloud-light texture. Because we're a little extra, we go bicolor, with a layer of milk chocolate mousse capping a layer of bittersweet. (With a technique so easy, what's to lose?) Both mousses are held in a graham cracker crust and topped with the easiest-ever chocolate curl confetti.

8 **graham crackers**, finely crushed

3 tablespoons **unsalted butter**, melted

2 cups **bittersweet chocolate chips**

3 cups **whipped cream**

2 cups **milk chocolate chips**

1 (2-ounce) bar **dark chocolate**

2 tablespoons **unsweetened cocoa powder**

1 In a medium bowl, stir together the graham cracker crumbs and melted butter until the crumbs are evenly moistened. Transfer the crumbs to an 8-inch springform pan and use the bottom of a measuring cup to press them into an even layer over the bottom.

2 Place the bittersweet chocolate chips in a medium heatproof bowl and microwave on high power for 1 minute, until just melted. Set aside to cool to room temperature, about 10 minutes. Using a rubber spatula, fold 1½ cups of the whipped cream into the cooled melted chocolate until evenly combined. Pour the dark chocolate mousse over the crust and smooth the top with the spatula. Freeze for 15 minutes to quickly firm the mousse.

3 Meanwhile, place the milk chocolate chips in a medium heatproof bowl and microwave on high power for 1 minute, until just melted. Set aside to cool to room temperature, about 10 minutes. Fold the remaining 1½ cups whipped cream into the cooled melted chocolate until evenly combined. Pour the milk chocolate mousse over the dark chocolate mousse and smooth out the top. Freeze for 2 hours, or until both layers of mousse are set.

4 Using a vegetable peeler, shave off chocolate curls from the long side of the chocolate bar. Make at least 2 tablespoons of curls.

5 Remove the tart from the freezer and gently remove the outer ring of the springform pan. Sift the cocoa powder evenly over the top of the tart, then sprinkle with the chocolate shavings. Transfer the tart to a serving plate or cake stand. Cut into wedges and serve chilled.

THREE-INGREDIENT

CHOCOLATE-HAZELNUT MUG CAKES

If you think there's nothing better than polishing off a jar of chocolate-hazelnut spread with a spoon, prepare to freak out: Because when you mix in a couple of eggs and a touch of flour, you suddenly have a batter that'll turn into a tender, spoonable cake in literally two microwave minutes. It's fast enough to make no matter how worn down you're feeling.

¾ cup **chocolate-hazelnut spread**, such as Nutella, plus more for frosting

2 large **eggs**

¼ cup **all-purpose flour**

1 In a medium bowl, whisk together the chocolate-hazelnut spread and eggs until smooth. Stir in the flour until just combined.

2 Divide the batter between two 6-ounce microwave-safe mugs. Microwave both mugs together on high power for 2 minutes, until the mixture is puffed and cooked through.

3 Remove the mugs from the microwave and let cool for 1 minute.

4 Frost each cake with a large spoonful of chocolate-hazelnut spread and serve warm.

CHOCOLATE PEANUT BUTTER
LAVA CAKES

Is there a more dynamic duo than chocolate and peanut butter? In this impressive recipe, peanut butter cups meet '90s-style molten lava cakes, which means that the pool of chocolate that normally gushes out when you reach the center has been replaced by liquid peanut butter. Swap in a nut butter that you love or one that's staring you down from the depths of your pantry: Just be sure it's similar in consistency to smooth peanut butter (totally homogenized and not too grainy).

½ cup (1 stick) **unsalted butter**, plus more for greasing

Unsweetened Dutch-processed cocoa powder, for dusting

4 ounces **bittersweet chocolate**, finely chopped, plus more for garnish

⅓ cup **granulated sugar**

1 teaspoon **vanilla extract**

½ teaspoon **kosher salt**

3 large **eggs**

½ cup smooth **peanut butter**

Vanilla ice cream, for serving

1 Preheat the oven to 425°F. Grease four 8-ounce ramekins with butter, then dust them with cocoa powder to coat and tap out any excess.

2 In a medium heatproof bowl, combine the butter and chocolate and microwave on high power for about 1½ minutes, stirring every 15 seconds, until fully melted and well combined. Set aside to cool for 10 minutes.

3 In a separate medium bowl, whisk together the sugar, vanilla, salt, and eggs. Add the cooled melted chocolate mixture and stir until smooth.

4 Place the prepared ramekins on a rimmed baking sheet. Pour ¼ cup of the batter into each ramekin, then place about 2 tablespoons of the peanut butter in the center of each ramekin. Top each with another ¼ cup of the batter to cover the peanut butter. Bake until the sides are firm but the centers are still soft, 10 to 12 minutes. Remove the baking sheet from the oven.

5 Working with one ramekin at a time and using a kitchen towel to hold them, place an individual serving plate on top of a ramekin and invert the cake onto the plate, gently shaking the ramekin to loosen the cake if needed. Repeat to unmold the remaining cakes.

6 Top each cake with a scoop of vanilla ice cream, sprinkle with some finely chopped chocolate, and serve hot.

FLOURLESS
CHOCOLATE TORTE

If you're looking to impress your friends with your pastry chops, look no further: Nearly every great dessert master has their own version of this flourless chocolate torte (read: dense, low-slung cake), which relies on almond flour to hold all of the chocolate together, and whipped egg whites, not baking powder or baking soda, to lift it up. Naturally gluten-free, it's classic enough to be the little black dress of chocolate desserts, appropriate for any occasion and always flattering. Two tips for success: Make sure your almond flour is superfine (you can press it through a fine-mesh sieve to get rid of the clumps), and fold in the meringue with a gentle hand to avoid deflating it.

¾ cup (1½ sticks) **unsalted butter**, cubed, at room temperature, plus more for greasing

1¾ cups **superfine almond flour**

8 ounces **dark chocolate** (preferably 60 to 70% cacao), coarsely chopped

1½ teaspoons **kosher salt**

1 cup **granulated sugar**

1 tablespoon **vanilla extract**

6 large **eggs**, separated

Confectioners' sugar, for garnish

Whipped cream, for serving (optional)

1 Preheat the oven to 375°F. Grease a 9-inch springform pan with butter, then dust it with ⅓ cup of the almond flour to coat and tap out any excess.

2 In a medium bowl, microwave the chocolate on high power, stirring every 30 seconds, until melted and smooth. Set aside to cool for 10 minutes.

3 Combine the butter, salt, and ¾ cup of the granulated sugar in a large bowl. Using a handheld mixer, beat on medium-high speed until fluffy, 2 to 3 minutes. Add the vanilla and egg yolks and beat until smooth. Pour in the chocolate and beat until combined. Add the remaining almond flour and stir with a rubber spatula until evenly combined.

4 Place the egg whites in a separate large bowl. Using the handheld mixer with clean beaters, beat on medium-high speed until soft peaks form. Sprinkle in the remaining ¼ cup sugar and beat until stiff peaks form and the meringue is shiny.

5 Spoon one-quarter of the meringue into the chocolate batter and stir to combine and lighten the batter. Add the remaining meringue and use a rubber spatula to gently fold it into the batter until there are no visible streaks and the batter is smooth.

6 Scrape the batter into the prepared pan and smooth out the top with the rubber spatula (do not tap or knock the pan on the counter or the batter will lose the air it needs to rise). Bake for 20 minutes, then reduce the oven temperature to 350°F and bake until a toothpick inserted into the center of the cake comes out with a few crumbs attached, about 50 minutes more.

7 Transfer the pan to a wire rack and let the cake cool completely, about 3 hours. The cake will sink in the middle and crack on top.

8 Remove the outer ring of the springform pan and place the cake on a serving plate. Dust the top with confectioners' sugar and serve with whipped cream alongside, if you like.

GERMAN CHOCOLATE
PUDDING PARFAITS

Old-school German chocolate cake—layers of chocolate pastry with coconut-pecan frosting—has nothing to do with the country of lederhosen and Oktoberfest. Its name is actually derived from "German's Sweet Chocolate," a baking chocolate that can be traced back to the 1850s and is named for its American inventor, Sam German. The recipe for the cake itself didn't come until a century later, when it was published in a Texas newspaper. It's been another fifty years since then, and we're due for an update: In this recipe, we're layering pudding, custard, whipped cream, and toasted coconut and pecans for a cooler, creamier dessert. If you can't find German's chocolate, swap semi-sweet in its place; your dessert will be slightly less sweet, but just as delicious.

CUSTARD

¾ cup **granulated sugar**

2 large **egg yolks**

¾ cup **evaporated milk**

6 tablespoons (¾ stick) **unsalted butter**, melted

1 teaspoon **vanilla extract**

PUDDING

⅔ cup **granulated sugar**

2 tablespoons **cornstarch**

½ teaspoon **kosher salt**

6 large **egg yolks**

3 cups **whole milk**

10 ounces **German's chocolate**, coarsely chopped

2 tablespoons **unsalted butter**, cubed

1 teaspoon **vanilla extract**

TOPPING

1½ cups whole **pecans**

1½ cups **unsweetened flaked coconut**

2 cups chilled **heavy cream**

German's chocolate, for grating (optional)

1 Make the custard sauce: In a medium saucepan, whisk together the granulated sugar and egg yolks until they form a thick paste, then stir in the evaporated milk, butter, and vanilla. Place the pan over medium heat and cook, stirring often, until the custard has thickened enough to coat the back of the spoon, 8 to 9 minutes. Transfer the sauce to a bowl (set the pan aside) and let cool for 30 minutes. Cover the custard with plastic wrap, pressing directly against the custard to prevent a skin from forming, and refrigerate for at least 2 hours and up to 1 day.

2 Meanwhile, make the German chocolate pudding: Rinse out and dry the saucepan you used for the custard sauce. Place the granulated sugar, cornstarch, and salt in the pan and whisk to combine. Add the egg yolks and stir until the mixture forms a thick paste. Pour in the milk and whisk until smooth. Set the pan over medium heat and cook, stirring continuously, until the mixture begins to bubble and thicken, 12 to 14 minutes. Remove the pan from the heat and add the chocolate, butter, and vanilla. Stir until the chocolate and butter have melted and the mixture is smooth. Pour the pudding through a fine-

(recipe continues)

mesh strainer into a large bowl, pressing it through with a rubber spatula. Cover the bowl with plastic wrap, pressing it directly against the surface of the pudding to prevent a skin from forming, and refrigerate the pudding until completely chilled and set, at least 4 hours or up to overnight.

3 Make the topping: Preheat the oven to 350°F.

4 Spread the pecans over a rimmed baking sheet and bake until toasted and fragrant, 8 to 10 minutes. Transfer the pecans to a cutting board, let cool, then coarsely chop. Spread the coconut flakes over the same baking sheet and bake until lightly toasted and fragrant, 6 to 8 minutes, stirring once halfway through. Transfer the coconut to a bowl, let cool, then stir in the chopped pecans.

5 In a large bowl, whisk the cream until stiff peaks form.

6 Assemble the parfaits: Arrange eight 8-ounce (or larger) jars or glasses on a rimmed baking sheet. Spoon 1 tablespoon of the pecan-coconut mixture into each glass, then drizzle each with 1 tablespoon of the custard sauce. Spoon ¼ cup of the pudding into each glass, followed by 2 tablespoons of the whipped cream. Repeat the layering one more time, then sprinkle the remaining pecan-coconut mixture on top of each parfait.

7 Using a Microplane or vegetable peeler, grate more German's chocolate over the top of each parfait if you like. Serve immediately or refrigerate for up to 4 hours before serving.

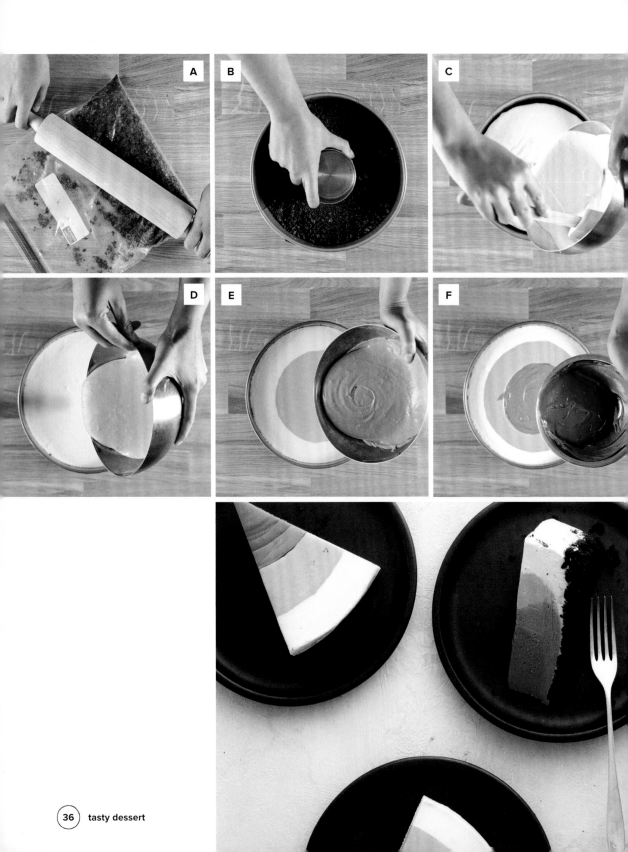

tasty dessert

CHOCOLATE RIPPLE
CHEESECAKE

We took everything that makes a cheesecake intimidating—we're looking at you, precarious water bath and high risk of ravine-like cracks—and tossed it out the window. And that left us with a towering no-bake, no-fuss cheesecake, for absolutely no trouble at all. How? This cheesecake is set not with eggs but with gelatin for a reliable firmness that doesn't require any oven time, just a chill in the fridge. But what really makes this a showstopper is the chocolate ombré—simple to execute and stunning to behold.

24 **chocolate cookies**, such as Nabisco Famous Chocolate Wafers

4 tablespoons (½ stick) **unsalted butter**, melted

2 cups **heavy cream**

1 tablespoon unflavored **powdered gelatin**

4 (8-ounce) packages **cream cheese**, at room temperature

¾ cup **granulated sugar**

1 teaspoon **vanilla extract**

½ cup **semisweet chocolate chips**

1 Place the cookies in a gallon-size zip-top plastic bag and use a rolling pin to crush them into fine crumbs **A**. Pour the crumbs into a medium bowl. Add the melted butter and stir until the crumbs are evenly moistened.

2 Transfer the crumbs to a 9-inch springform pan and use a measuring cup to press them into an even layer over the bottom of the pan **B**. Refrigerate the crust to set while you make the fillings.

3 Pour the cream into a medium heatproof bowl or liquid measuring cup, then stir in the gelatin. Let stand to soften the gelatin, at least 5 minutes. Microwave the mixture on high power for 1 minute, until warm to the touch. Stir the cream until the gelatin has dissolved.

4 Combine the cream cheese, sugar, and vanilla in a large bowl. Using a handheld mixer, beat on medium speed until smooth, 1 minute. Add the cream-gelatin mixture and beat on low speed until the sugar has dissolved and the mixture is smooth, about 1 minute.

5 Pour 2¼ cups of the batter over the crust **C**. Pour ¾ cup of the batter into a small bowl and divide the remaining 3 cups batter between two medium bowls. Melt the chocolate chips in a heatproof bowl in the microwave until smooth.

6 Add 1 tablespoon of the melted chocolate to one medium bowl of batter and stir until smooth. Add 3 tablespoons of the melted chocolate to the second medium bowl of batter and stir until smooth. Add 2 tablespoons of the melted chocolate to the small bowl of batter and stir until smooth. The color of the batter in each bowl should be darker than the last.

7 Slowly pour the lightest-colored batter into the center of the plain batter in the pan **D**. Repeat with the medium-colored batter **E**, then the darkest batter **F**. Lightly tap the bottom of the pan against the counter to settle the batters and smooth the top, then refrigerate the cheesecake for at least 4 hours or up to 12 hours, until set.

8 Remove the outer ring of the springform pan and transfer the cheesecake to a serving plate. Cut into wedges and serve chilled.

ORANGE—CHOCOLATE GANACHE TART

It's not cool to invite your friends over and serve them the chocolate orange you get in your Christmas stocking. It *is* cool to invite them over and serve a dessert that's inspired by that treat you all secretly love but with dynamic textures (crumbly crust! fudgy ganache! juicy fruit!), a photo-worthy presentation, and no foil wrapper. You'll pick up a lot of skills as you make this tart—like blind-baking a crust, creating a ganache, and segmenting an orange—that will serve you well in future baking endeavors. Consider them like scout badges.

CRUST

1¼ cups **all-purpose flour**, plus more for dusting

¼ cup **unsweetened Dutch-processed cocoa powder**

½ teaspoon **kosher salt**

Finely grated zest of 1 **orange**

⅓ cup **vegetable shortening**, chilled

⅓ cup ice-cold **water**

GANACHE

8 ounces **bittersweet chocolate** (70 to 80% cacao), coarsely chopped

1 teaspoon **vanilla extract**

½ teaspoon **kosher salt**

¾ cup fresh **orange juice**

TOPPING

⅓ cup **orange marmalade**

4 **oranges**, peeled and cut into segments

Whipped cream, for serving

1 Make the crust: In a food processor, combine the flour, cocoa powder, salt, and orange zest and pulse until evenly combined. Add the shortening and pulse until pea-size crumbles form, about 10 pulses. Add the water and pulse until the dough is evenly moistened and starts to clump together, about 10 pulses. Scrape the dough out onto a clean work surface and pat it into a ½-inch-thick disc. Wrap the disc in plastic wrap and refrigerate for about 1 hour.

2 On a lightly floured work surface, roll out the dough into a 12-inch circle, about ⅛ inch thick. Transfer the dough circle to a 9½-inch tart pan with a removable bottom or a 9-inch pie pan, pressing it gently into the bottom and up the sides of the pan. Trim the dough so it's flush with the edge of the pan **A** . Refrigerate the dough for 30 minutes.

3 Preheat the oven to 375°F.

4 Tear off a 12-inch square of parchment paper and crumple it into a ball. Flatten the parchment sheet and place it over the dough in the tart pan. Pour in 3 cups pie weights (see page 19) and spread them into an even layer **B** . Bake until the crust is no longer shiny at the edges, about 15 minutes. Carefully lift the parchment sheet with the weights out of the pan. Bake until the crust is completely cooked through, about 15 minutes more. Transfer the pan to a wire rack and set aside while you make the ganache.

5 Make the ganache: In a medium heatproof bowl, combine the chocolate, vanilla, and salt. In a small saucepan, bring the orange juice to a simmer over high heat, then pour it over the chocolate. Let the chocolate stand, undisturbed, for 1 minute, then use a small rubber spatula or spoon to slowly stir from the center to the edges until the chocolate has melted completely and the mixture is smooth and well combined. Pour the ganache into the crust **C** and smooth out the top with a rubber spatula. Refrigerate for about 2 hours, or until the ganache is set.

6 Make the topping: Place the marmalade in a medium bowl and microwave on high power for 20 to 30 seconds, until loosened and barely warm. Add the orange segments (discard any juice) and toss gently to coat.

7 Using a fork as an aide, arrange the orange segments in concentric circles on top of the ganache, beginning from the outside and working your way toward the center, until the ganache is completely covered **D**. Refrigerate the tart for about 30 minutes to set the marmalade.

8 To serve, remove the outer ring of the tart pan and transfer the tart to a serving plate. Cut into wedges and serve cold, with whipped cream alongside.

MISSISSIPPI MUD PIE

When you're having an "I want it all and I want it now" moment, three-in-one Mississippi Mud Pie is here to save the day. Chocolate pudding tops a fudgy brownie, both of which sit in a crisp and crumbly chocolate cookie crust. The whole triple-threat chocolate bonanza is blanketed in a layer of soft whipped cream (not *everything* can be chocolate), then dusted with more cocoa powder for good measure (and to appease the chocolate gods, upset by our last parenthetical).

CRUST

Nonstick cooking spray

2 cups **chocolate cookie crumbs** (from 30 cookies, such as Nabisco Famous Chocolate Wafers)

½ cup (1 stick) **unsalted butter**, melted and cooled

BROWNIE

8 ounces **dark chocolate** (preferably 70 to 80% cacao), coarsely chopped

1 cup (2 sticks) **unsalted butter**

1 cup packed **dark brown sugar**

1 cup **granulated sugar**

2 teaspoons **vanilla extract**

½ teaspoon **kosher salt**

4 large **eggs**

1 cup **all-purpose flour**

PUDDING

¾ cup **granulated sugar**

⅓ cup **unsweetened natural cocoa powder**

⅓ cup **all-purpose flour**

½ teaspoon **kosher salt**

2 large **egg yolks**

2 cups **whole milk**

2 tablespoons **unsalted butter**, cubed and chilled

1½ teaspoons **vanilla extract**

1 cup chilled **heavy cream**

1 Make the crust: Preheat the oven to 350°F. Coat a 9-inch springform pan with cooking spray and line the inside of the springform ring with a strip of parchment paper, trimming it flush with the top of the pan.

2 In a large bowl, stir together the cookie crumbs and melted butter until the crumbs are evenly moistened. Transfer the crumbs to the prepared pan and use the bottom of a measuring cup to press them into an even layer over the bottom of the pan. Set the pan aside while you make the brownie layer.

3 Make the brownie layer: In a large glass bowl, combine the chocolate and butter and microwave on high power, stirring every 30 seconds, until melted and smooth.

4 In a separate large bowl, whisk together the brown sugar, granulated sugar, vanilla, salt, and eggs until lightened in color and foamy, about 1 minute. Pour in the melted chocolate mixture and whisk until smooth. Add the flour and stir until just combined.

5 Pour the batter over the crust and smooth out the top with a rubber spatula. Bake until a toothpick inserted halfway between the center and the edge comes out clean, about 30 minutes.

6 Meanwhile, make the pudding layer: In a medium saucepan, whisk together the granulated sugar, cocoa powder, flour, and salt until combined. Add the egg yolks and a splash of the milk and stir until the

mixture forms a thick, smooth paste. Add the remaining milk and whisk until smooth. Set the pan over medium heat and cook, stirring continuously, until the mixture starts to bubble and thicken, 8 to 10 minutes. Remove the pan from the heat, add the butter and vanilla, and stir until the butter has melted and the mixture is smooth and well combined.

7 When the brownie layer is ready, transfer the pan to a wire rack, pour the warm pudding over the brownie layer, and smooth out the top with a rubber spatula. Let cool to room temperature, about 1 hour. Cover and refrigerate for at least 4 hours or up to 1 day.

8 When ready to serve, whisk the cream in a large bowl until it forms stiff peaks.

9 Remove the pie from the refrigerator. Remove the outer ring of the springform pan, then peel away and discard the strip of parchment paper and set the pie on a serving plate. Spread the whipped cream over the top of the pie, and dust with additional cocoa powder. Serve the pie chilled.

"PLATINUM" BLONDIES

White chocolate lovers, wave your flag high. So it may be a little milder, milkier, and more buttery than bittersweet, but sometimes you just need that uncomplicated comfort. These blondies are just as gooey as our ultimate brownies and, since white chocolate lovers tend to really love white chocolate, they've got a white chocolate topping, too. If you really, really love white chocolate (like, you dream of bathing in it), dip every single blondie in melted white chocolate for a crunchy shell on all sides.

1 cup **vegetable oil**, plus more for greasing

2 cups **all-purpose flour**, plus more for dusting

1½ pounds high-quality **white chocolate** (not chips), coarsely chopped

1½ cups **granulated sugar**

5 large **egg whites**, at room temperature

2 teaspoons **vanilla extract**

1 teaspoon **kosher salt**

1 Preheat the oven to 325°F. Lightly grease a 9 by 13-inch baking pan with vegetable oil, then dust it with flour to coat and tap out any excess.

2 Place 8 ounces of the white chocolate in a medium heatproof bowl and microwave on 50 percent power, stirring every 30 seconds, until melted and smooth. Set aside to cool for 5 minutes.

3 In a large bowl, whisk together the sugar and egg whites until lightened in texture and foamy on top, about 1 minute. Add the vegetable oil, vanilla, and salt and whisk until smooth. Scrape in the melted white chocolate and whisk until just combined. Add the flour and stir with a wooden spoon until evenly combined.

4 Scrape the batter into the prepared pan and smooth out the top with the rubber spatula. Bake until a toothpick inserted halfway between the center and the edge comes out clean, 30 to 35 minutes. Transfer the pan to a wire rack and let the blondies cool to room temperature.

5 Turn the blondies out of the pan onto a baking sheet, then invert them onto a cutting board so they're right side up. Cut into 2-inch squares.

6 Place the remaining 1 pound white chocolate in a medium heatproof bowl and microwave on 50 percent power, stirring every 30 seconds, until melted and smooth. Set aside to cool for 5 minutes.

7 Dip or spread the top of each blondie in the melted white chocolate, or use two forks to coat them completely in the white chocolate, transferring them to a sheet of parchment as you go. Let the blondies stand until the white chocolate has set before serving.

CRUNCHY, CRACKLY, CRISPY

honeycomb toffee

makes about 24 candies

Imagine pure caramel flavor that comes not in the form of candy that's toffee-sticky or brittle-sharp, but instead in shards that are impossibly crunchy and light, with pockets of air that make each piece look like coral reef or the foam that washes up with the waves. We're describing honeycomb candy (also known as sea foam, sponge candy, and cinder toffee), which is outrageously addictive and makes any just-creamy dessert more interesting. Honeycomb gets its characteristic spongy-crunch from baking soda, which makes the sugar syrup puff up rapidly (just like those volcanoes you made in kindergarten). Beware: Humidity's the enemy of honeycomb. Be sure to store the finished product in an airtight container at room temperature.

Nonstick cooking spray

1 teaspoon **baking soda**

1 teaspoon **vanilla extract**

2 cups **granulated sugar**

⅓ cup **light corn syrup**

3 tablespoons **honey**

1 Coat a 9 by 13-inch baking pan with cooking spray. Line the bottom and all four sides with parchment paper, leaving 1 inch of overhang all around. Coat the parchment thoroughly with cooking spray.

2 In a small bowl, stir together the baking soda and vanilla.

3 In a large saucepan, combine the sugar, corn syrup, honey, and ⅓ cup water. Attach a candy thermometer to the side of the pan and heat over medium-high heat, stirring to dissolve the sugar, until the mixture comes to a boil. Once the syrup begins to boil, stop stirring and cook until the syrup registers 300°F on the candy thermometer.

4 Remove the pan from the heat. Working quickly, stir the baking soda and vanilla together again, then pour the mixture into the pan with the syrup and stir with a wooden spoon until the syrup bubbles up like fluff and expands. Quickly pour the bubbling syrup evenly into the prepared pan—do not move the pan or try to spread the syrup evenly, or you will deflate the bubbles that give the toffee its characteristic lightness and crunch. Let the toffee cool completely, undisturbed, 1 to 2 hours.

5 Using the parchment paper as handles, lift the cooled toffee from the pan and set it on a cutting board. Using a wooden spoon, the heel of a knife, or another blunt object, crack the toffee into bite-size pieces. Store the toffee in an airtight container at room temperature for up to 3 days.

TASTY WAYS TO ENJOY

* Sprinkle over frosting between cake layers
  for a crunchy layer cake

* Sprinkle over ice cream sundaes as a topping

* Sprinkle over melted chocolate to make bark candy

* Fold into ice cream for no-bake ice cream cake

* Layer in glasses with pudding and whipped
  cream for crunchy parfaits

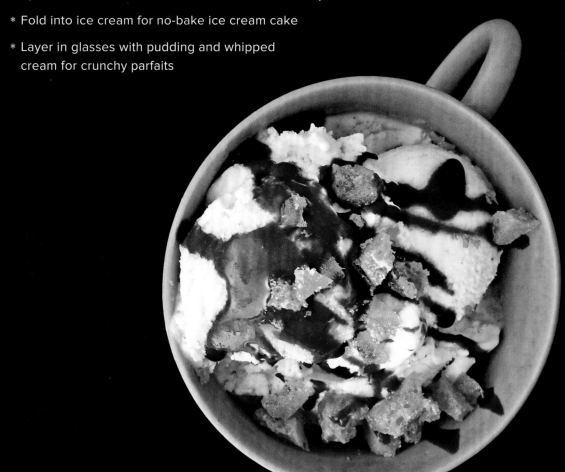

"1,000 LAYERS"
PUFF PASTRY STACK

In French, the name for this crunchy-creamy dessert is *mille-feuille* (pronounced "mee foy"), which translates into "thousand leaves," a reference to magical puff pastry that unfurls into layer upon layer of crispy, buttery dough in the oven. Three sheets of puff are broiled with sugar to make a caramel cover, then stacked with a dead-simple vanilla pastry cream (made in the microwave, praise be!) and sliced strawberries. *Très élégant!* One day when you have a ton of time (and butter), you can make puff pastry at home, but when you're in need of a same-day dessert that's just as sophisticated, the store-bought kind will do the trick.

½ cup plus 1 tablespoon **granulated sugar**

3 large **egg yolks**

3 tablespoons **cornstarch**

1½ cups **whole milk**

1½ teaspoons **vanilla extract**

1 (9-inch-square) sheet frozen **puff pastry**, thawed

6 fresh **strawberries**, thinly sliced

Confectioners' sugar, for dusting

1 In a medium heatproof bowl, whisk together ½ cup of the granulated sugar and the egg yolks until pale in color, about 1 minute. Add the cornstarch and whisk until smooth, then add the milk and vanilla and whisk again until evenly combined. Loosely cover the bowl with plastic wrap and microwave the mixture on high power, stirring halfway through, until thickened, about 4 minutes. Remove the plastic wrap and stir to smooth the pudding. Cover the bowl with the plastic wrap and refrigerate until the pudding is chilled and set, about 1 hour.

2 Preheat the oven to 400°F. Line a baking sheet with parchment paper.

3 Cut the thawed puff pastry along its fold lines into 3 equal-size rectangles. Place the puff pastry rectangles on the prepared baking sheet and pierce each piece all over with the tines of a fork. Bake the puff pastry rectangles until lightly risen, golden brown, and crisp, about 15 minutes. Remove the baking sheet from the oven and switch the oven to broil.

4 Sprinkle the remaining 1 tablespoon granulated sugar evenly over the rectangles, then broil until the sugar caramelizes like the topping on crème brûlée, 30 to 60 seconds (watch carefully to be sure the pastry doesn't burn). Transfer the baking sheet to a wire rack and let the rectangles cool completely.

5 About an hour before you plan to serve it, assemble the pastry stack: Transfer the pudding to a piping bag fitted with a large flat tip or a zip-top plastic bag with one corner snipped off. Place 1 puff pastry rectangle on a serving plate, sugared-side up, and pipe one-fourth of the pudding over the top. Arrange half the sliced strawberries over the pudding, then pipe another one-fourth of the pudding over the berries. Top with a second puff pastry rectangle, half the remaining pudding, the remaining sliced strawberries, the remaining pudding, and, finally, the remaining puff pastry rectangle.

6 Dust the top of the stack with confectioners' sugar and serve within the hour to ensure the pastry doesn't get soggy.

ICE CREAM
CHURRO BOWLS

Remember when it boggled your mind that soup could be served in an edible bread bowl? Well, we've taken the fried churro and turned it into a superb vessel for a scoop of ice cream (or two if you're a risk-taker). The outside is dusted in cinnamon-sugar and crisp as a fritter, ideal for softening up with melty ice cream.

4 tablespoons (½ stick) **unsalted butter**

2 tablespoons packed **light brown sugar**

½ teaspoon **kosher salt**

1 cup **all-purpose flour**

1 teaspoon **vanilla extract**

4 large **eggs**

Nonstick cooking spray

Vegetable oil, for frying

1 cup **granulated sugar**

2 tablespoons ground **cinnamon**

Vanilla ice cream, for serving

Hot fudge sauce and **caramel sauce**, for serving

1 In a medium saucepan, combine the butter, brown sugar, salt, and 1 cup water and, bring to a boil over high heat, stirring occasionally to dissolve the sugar. Add the flour all at once, reduce the heat to medium, and cook, stirring continuously with a wooden spoon, until the dough forms a ball and easily pulls away from the side of the pan **A**, about 1 minute. Remove the pan from the heat and let the dough cool for 5 minutes.

2 Add the vanilla and 1 of the eggs and stir until fully incorporated into the dough, then add the remaining 3 eggs **B**, one at a time, stirring until each is incorporated before adding the next. The dough is ready when it forms a "V" shape as you lift the spoon out of the dough. Transfer the dough to a piping bag fitted with a ⅜-inch star tip.

3 Set a 12-cup muffin tin upside down on a large baking sheet and coat it thoroughly with cooking spray. Starting at the base of each cup and working toward the top, pipe the dough around the inverted cups to form 8 bowls **C**. Transfer the baking sheet to the freezer and freeze until the dough is solid, at least 3 hours or up to overnight.

4 Fill a large Dutch oven or heavy pot with vegetable oil to a depth of 2 inches. Attach a deep-fry thermometer to the side and heat the oil over high heat to 350°F. Line a baking sheet with paper towels and set it nearby. In a medium bowl, whisk together the granulated sugar and cinnamon.

5 Remove the muffin tin from the freezer and flex it to release the dough bowls. (You may need to insert the tip of a table knife under the bottom edge of each cup to pry them free.) Return 6 of the bowls to the freezer. Carefully place the remaining 2 bowls into the hot oil and fry, turning them with tongs or a spider, until golden brown and cooked through, about 3 minutes. Transfer the bowls to the prepared baking sheet to drain briefly, then, while they're still hot, toss them in the bowl of cinnamon sugar until fully coated. Transfer the bowls to a wire rack to cool completely. Repeat with the remaining bowls, working in batches of two.

6 When ready to serve, fill each bowl with scoops of ice cream and drizzle with hot fudge and caramel sauce.

CHOCOLATE SWIRL MERINGUES

One taste of homemade meringues and you'll never go back to the store-bought kind. Unlike the ones your granny used to keep around (chalky and dry all the way through), these have a crunchy shell that'll break into a million pieces and a gooey, almost marshmallow center. Plus, they're just chocolatey enough to keep you coming back for more. Make sure you take your egg white–sugar mixture alllll the way to stiff peaks: The meringue should hold its shape when you lift the whisk out of the bowl, with a tippy-top that doesn't bend or flop.

3 large **egg whites**

¾ cup **granulated sugar**

1 tablespoon **vanilla extract**

½ teaspoon **white wine vinegar**

⅔ cup **bittersweet chocolate chips**, melted and cooled

Fresh berries, for serving (optional)

1 Preheat the oven to 200°F. Line a large baking sheet with parchment paper.

2 Place the egg whites in a large bowl. Using a handheld mixer, beat on medium-high speed until soft peaks form. With the mixer running, slowly pour in the sugar and beat until stiff peaks form. Add the vanilla and vinegar and beat until evenly incorporated.

3 Pour the melted chocolate over the meringue and use a large rubber spatula to gently swirl it into the meringue until halfway combined (you want the final meringues to be marbled).

4 Using a large serving spoon, spoon the meringue onto the prepared baking sheet in 6 large heaping mounds. Bake until the meringues are dry to the touch, about 2 hours. Turn the oven off and leave the meringues inside to cool completely, about 2 hours, without opening the oven door.

5 Peel the cooled meringues off the parchment paper with your hands or a flat metal spatula and set them on a serving plate. Serve with fresh berries, if you like.

CRISPY-CRUSTED
CHOCOLATE CHEESECAKE

There is no shame in the pleasure of a pure, unadulterated cereal treat, with its gooey strands of marshmallow and crispy edges that splinter into delicious crumbs. But to take it to the next level, use it as the base for a lush chocolate cheesecake. It'll do a much better job than a cookie crust of staying snappy, crackly, and poppy.

4 tablespoons (½ stick) **unsalted butter**, plus more for greasing

1 (10-ounce) bag **mini marshmallows**

6 cups crispy **rice cereal**, such as Rice Krispies

8 ounces **semisweet chocolate**, finely chopped

¼ cup **heavy cream**

2 (8-ounce) packages **cream cheese**, at room temperature

½ cup **granulated sugar**

1 teaspoon **vanilla extract**

1½ cups **whipped cream**, plus more for garnish

1 (2-ounce) **milk chocolate bar**, for garnish

1 Grease the bottom of a measuring cup with butter.

2 In a large saucepan, melt the butter over medium heat. Add the marshmallows and stir until they have completely melted and the mixture is well combined. Add the rice cereal and stir until well coated. Transfer the cereal mixture to a 10-inch springform pan and use the greased measuring cup to press it into a ½-inch-thick layer over the bottom and up the side of the pan while the cereal mixture is warm.

3 In a small heatproof bowl, combine the chocolate and heavy cream and microwave on high power for about 1 minute, stirring once halfway through, until melted and well combined.

4 Combine the cream cheese, sugar, and vanilla in a large bowl. Using a handheld mixer, beat on medium speed until smooth, about 1 minute. Pour in the melted chocolate mixture and beat until evenly incorporated. Add the whipped cream and use a rubber spatula to gently fold it into the batter until smooth.

5 Pour the batter into the crust and smooth out the top with the rubber spatula. Cover and refrigerate until the cheesecake is set, at least 4 hours or up to overnight.

6 Cover the top of the cheesecake with more whipped cream, then use a vegetable peeler to shave the milk chocolate over the whipped cream. Cut into wedges and serve chilled.

CHOCOLATE CRUNCH BARK

The beauty of breaking this bark into "bite-size" servings is that you get to decide just how big those bites are. And we're guessing you'll go back for seconds of these salty crackers layered with butterscotch sauce, melted chocolate, and roughly chopped pecans, no matter how big you make each piece. The recipe makes a big batch, which means you can keep a stash in the freezer and sneak a handful all week long. Passover observers: If you replace the saltines with matzo and use kosher-for-Passover ingredients, this bark is Seder-ready.

4½ ounces **saltine crackers** (about 52)

1 cup (2 sticks) **unsalted butter**

1 cup plus 2 tablespoons packed **light brown sugar**

2 cups **semisweet chocolate chips**

½ cup whole **pecans**, toasted and coarsely chopped

1 Preheat the oven to 350°F. Line a large rimmed baking sheet with parchment paper.

2 Arrange the crackers in a single layer on the prepared baking sheet so that the entire surface is covered, breaking them to fit if needed.

3 Melt the butter in a small saucepan over medium heat. Stir in the brown sugar, bring to a simmer, and cook, stirring, until smooth, about 3 minutes. Immediately pour the butter mixture evenly over the crackers and spread it with a spatula to cover them all.

4 Bake the crackers for 5 minutes. Remove the baking sheet from the oven and sprinkle the chocolate chips evenly over the crackers. Cover the baking sheet with foil to trap in the heat and let stand for 3 minutes to soften the chocolate. Remove the foil and use a rubber spatula to spread the softened chocolate evenly over the crackers. Sprinkle the pecans over the chocolate, then transfer the baking sheet to the freezer. Freeze until the bark is set, at least 1 hour or up to 1 day.

5 Break up the bark into bite-size pieces and serve chilled. Store any remaining bark in an airtight container in the freezer for up to 5 days.

CORNMEAL AND BERRY JAM
CRUMB BARS

makes 12 bars

These jam bars, ideal for a bake sale, picnic, or long car ride, are a dose of summer at any time of year. You'll make a crust that's crunchy from cornmeal, spread your favorite jam over the top, and then sprinkle on some reserved dough for a crumbly topping. Cut them into thick bars, asking your friends if they'd prefer a crisp edge piece, where the jam has caramelized in the pan, or a softer, fruitier middle section.

1 cup (2 sticks) **unsalted butter**, at room temperature, plus more for greasing

¼ cup **all-purpose flour**, plus more for dusting

1 cup **granulated sugar**

1 teaspoon **vanilla extract**

½ teaspoon **kosher salt**

2½ cups fine **cornmeal**

½ cup **mixed berry, blueberry, raspberry, or strawberry jam**

1   Grease a 9 by 13-inch metal baking pan with butter, then line the bottom and the two long sides with a sheet of parchment paper, leaving 1 inch overhanging the sides of the pan. Grease the parchment with butter, then dust it with flour to coat and tap out any excess.

2   Combine the butter, sugar, vanilla, and salt in a large bowl. Using a handheld mixer, beat on medium-high speed until light and fluffy, 2 to 3 minutes. Add the cornmeal and beat on low speed until just combined.

3   Transfer three-quarters of the dough to the prepared pan and use the bottom of a measuring cup to press it into an even layer over the bottom of the pan. Place the pan in the refrigerator. Add the flour to the dough remaining in the bowl and mix with your hands until it forms large crumbles. Place the crumbles in the refrigerator with the crust and chill for at least 30 minutes or up to 1 day.

4   Preheat the oven to 350°F.

5   Bake the crust until golden brown all over and no longer shiny, about 35 minutes. Remove the pan from the oven, pour the jam over the crust, and smooth it out into an even layer. Scatter the dough crumbles over the jam, then return the pan to the oven and bake until the crumbles are golden brown and the crust is firm, about 25 minutes. Transfer the pan to a wire rack and let the bars cool for 30 minutes.

6   Using the overhanging parchment paper as handles, lift the baked crust from the pan and set it on the wire rack. Remove the parchment paper and let the crust cool completely, about 2 hours. Cut into 12 bars to serve.

SALTED VANILLA BEAN
SHORTBREAD BARS

We're fans of sprinkles, cereal, and deep-frying, but here's proof that you don't always need theatrics to make a dessert that's dang good, plain and simple. Shortbread is a classic dessert for a reason, and no one is ever unhappy to see it: It's got a satisfying snap, yet it melts into buttery deliciousness as soon as it hits your tongue. This version is flavored with vanilla bean, which leaves beautiful flecks and a floral fragrance. Shortbread has a simple ingredient list and an even easier method—just make sure your butter-sugar mixture is well creamed (set a timer if you need to!).

Nonstick cooking spray

1½ cups **granulated sugar**

1 cup (2 sticks) **unsalted butter**, at room temperature

½ teaspoon **kosher salt**

½ **vanilla bean**, split lengthwise and seeds scraped out

3 cups **all-purpose flour**

1½ teaspoons **flaky sea salt**

1　Preheat the oven to 325°F. Coat a 9 by 13-inch metal baking pan with cooking spray, then line the bottom and two long sides with a sheet of parchment paper, leaving 1 inch overhanging the sides of the pan.

2　Combine the sugar, butter, kosher salt, and vanilla bean seeds in a large bowl. Using a handheld mixer, beat on medium speed until pale and very fluffy, about 6 minutes. Add the flour and beat on low speed until the mixture is just combined and no dry pockets of flour are visible.

3　Scrape the dough into the prepared pan and use the bottom of a measuring cup to press it into an even layer over the bottom of the pan. Using a paring knife, score the dough into 3 by ¾-inch rectangles. Sprinkle the dough evenly with the sea salt and press lightly to adhere it to the dough. Bake until the dough is golden brown all over and no longer shiny, about 1 hour.

4　Transfer the pan to a wire rack. Immediately cut the dough along the scored lines to separate the cookies. Let the cookies cool completely in the pan on the rack, about 1 hour.

5　Using the overhanging parchment paper as handles, lift the cookies out of the pan and set them on a cutting board. Separate the cookies fully from one another and serve or store in an airtight container at room temperature for up to 5 days.

CINNAMON TOAST
BISCOTTI

Biscotti are crunchy because they're baked not once but twice (in fact, the name means "twice-cooked"). First, you'll shape them in big, flipper-like logs and cook them until firm. Then, you'll slice those logs into long cookies and put back in the oven so that the insides crisp through. Because we can't leave good enough alone, we made our version even crunchier by sprinkling the cookies with coarse sugar and cinnamon to remind you of your favorite childhood breakfast cereal.

BISCOTTI

3 cups **all-purpose flour**

2 teaspoons **baking powder**

1 teaspoon **kosher salt**

1 cup **granulated sugar**

4 tablespoons (½ stick) **unsalted butter**, at room temperature

1 tablespoon ground **cinnamon**

2 large **eggs**

¼ cup **whole milk**

FINISHING

½ cup (1 stick) **unsalted butter**, melted

2 tablespoons **turbinado sugar**, such as Sugar In The Raw

2 teaspoons ground **cinnamon**

1 Preheat the oven to 325°F. Line two rimmed baking sheets with parchment paper.

2 Make the biscotti: In a medium bowl, whisk together the flour, baking powder, and salt.

3 Combine the granulated sugar, butter, and cinnamon in a large bowl. Using a handheld mixer, beat on medium-high speed until fluffy, 2 to 3 minutes. Add the eggs one at a time, beating well after each addition. Pour in the milk and beat until smooth. Add the flour mixture and beat on low speed until just combined.

4 Divide the dough in half and place one half on each prepared baking sheet. Form each half into a 3-inch-wide, 8½- to 9-inch-long flattened log. Refrigerate the dough on the baking sheets for 20 minutes.

5 Transfer both baking sheets to the oven and bake until the logs are lightly browned around the edges, 30 to 35 minutes, rotating the baking sheets from top to bottom and front to back halfway through the cooking time. Transfer the baking sheets to wire racks and let the logs cool for 15 minutes. Reduce the oven temperature to 300°F.

6 Finish the biscotti: Carefully transfer each log to a cutting board and, using a serrated knife, slice them crosswise into ½-inch-thick slices. Return the slices to the baking sheets, cut-side up and spaced evenly apart. Brush the slices on both sides with the melted butter, then sprinkle one side with the turbinado sugar and cinnamon. Bake until the biscotti are light brown at the edges and dry, 15 to 20 minutes, rotating the baking sheets from top to bottom and front to back halfway through the cooking time. Transfer the baking sheets to wire racks and let the biscotti cool to room temperature before serving. Store any remaining biscotti in an airtight container in the freezer for up to 5 days.

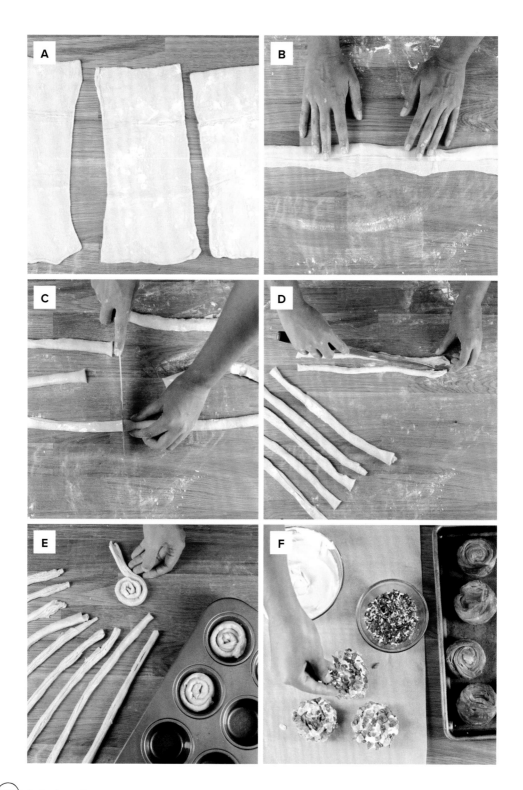

BIRTHDAY CAKE
PUFF PASTRY MUFFINS

We love a little high with a little low (sequins with silk and what-not), so a dessert where a golden-brown ruffle of puff pastry meets our favorite sprinkle-explosion boxed cake mix (you know the one) feels just right. Each little cake is shaped to expose as much of the buttery insides as possible and, once the pastry is shatteringly crunchy, it's dipped in milky white chocolate and coated in fruit cereal and sprinkles. And, pssst: If you only eat these on your birthday, you're missing out.

Nonstick cooking spray

1½ (9-inch-square) sheets frozen **puff pastry**, thawed

½ cup (1 stick) **unsalted butter**, at room temperature

1 large **egg**, whisked with 1 tablespoon **water**, for the egg wash

1 pound **white chocolate**, melted and cooled

1 cup **fruit cereal flakes**, such as Fruity Pebbles

1 cup **rainbow sprinkles** (optional)

1   Preheat the oven to 350°F. Coat a 12-cup muffin tin with cooking spray.

2   On a work surface, cut the whole puff pastry sheet in half so you have three half-pieces of pastry. Using a rolling pin, roll out each rectangle of puff pastry to a 24 by 8-inch rectangle A .

3   Brush each rectangle with one-third of the butter, then, starting from one long side, carefully roll each rectangle up into a tight log B . Cut each log in half crosswise to make 6 smaller logs C , then cut each in half lengthwise to make 12 half-logs D .

4   Working with one at a time, fold the smooth side of a half-log inward to create a spiraled snail-shell shape E and place it in one cup of the prepared muffin tin. Repeat with the remaining half-logs. Brush the top of each spiral with the egg wash.

5   Bake the puff pastry spirals until puffed, golden brown, and cooked through, about 30 minutes, rotating the pan once halfway through. Transfer the pan to a wire rack and let the spirals cool completely, at least 30 minutes.

6   Pour the white chocolate, fruit cereal, and sprinkles (if using) into individual bowls.

7   Dip the top of a cooled spiral in the melted white chocolate, letting the excess drip off completely, then dip in the cereal and sprinkles F . Set the spiral on a serving plate and repeat to coat the remaining spirals. Let the chocolate set for at least 30 minutes before serving.

BUTTER-PECAN
PALMIERS

Otherwise known as elephant ears (how cute is that?), palmiers are delicate, deceptively rich cookies made from puff pastry that's been rolled up with butter and sugar, which caramelize and crystallize in the oven. But we don't sprinkle the palmiers just with sugar—no, we use sugar that's nutty and toasty thanks to the addition of roasted and blitzed pecans. Once you've eaten a handful of palmiers on their own, prop a few into a generous scoop of butter-pecan ice cream for total mayhem.

1½ cups whole **pecans**

½ cup **granulated sugar**

½ teaspoon **kosher salt**

½ cup **turbinado sugar**, such as Sugar In The Raw

2 (9-inch-square) sheets frozen **puff pastry**, thawed in the refrigerator

½ cup (1 stick) **unsalted butter**, at room temperature

1   Preheat the oven to 350°F. Line two baking sheets with parchment paper.

2   Spread the pecans over an unlined rimmed baking sheet and bake until lightly toasted and fragrant, 8 to 10 minutes. Transfer the pecans to a cutting board and let cool; increase the oven temperature to 450°F. Transfer 1 cup of the cooled toasted pecans to a food processor. Finely chop the remaining ½ cup toasted pecans and set aside.

3   Add the granulated sugar and salt to the food processor and pulse until the pecans are finely ground with the sugar, about 30 pulses. Transfer the pecan sugar to a small bowl.

4   On a clean work surface, sprinkle ¼ cup of the pecan sugar evenly into a shape slightly larger than one puff pastry sheet, then sprinkle with 2 tablespoons of the turbinado sugar. Place one puff pastry sheet over the sugar mixture, then, using a rolling pin, roll the puff pastry into a 14-inch square, pressing the sugar mixture into the dough as you roll. Spread half the butter evenly over the pastry, then sprinkle it evenly with ¼ cup of the pecan sugar and 2 tablespoons of the turbinado sugar.

5   Fold two opposite sides of the square in toward each other so they come to the halfway point between the folded edge and the center of the square. Fold the sides in again so they just meet in the center. Finally, fold one side over the other like closing a book. Using a sharp knife, cut the log crosswise into ⅜-inch-thick slices. Transfer the slices to one of the prepared baking sheets, cut-side up and spaced 1 inch apart. Repeat with the remaining pecan sugar, turbinado sugar, puff pastry sheet, and butter and set the slices on the second prepared baking sheet. Sprinkle the slices evenly with the ½ cup finely chopped toasted pecans.

6   Bake until the palmiers are golden brown all over and puffed, 10 to 12 minutes, rotating the baking sheets from front to back and top to bottom halfway through the cooking time.

7   Transfer the baking sheets to wire racks and let cool for 5 minutes. Using a flat metal spatula, transfer the palmiers to the racks and let cool completely before serving. Store any remaining palmiers in an airtight container in the freezer for up to 5 days.

CHEWY

&

GOOEY

classic sugar cookies

There are some sturdy sugar cookies that exist mostly as a canvas for elaborate designs and crack sharply in two when you snap them in half. But these are not those kind of cookies. These crispy-edged, soft-centered classics will bend when you attempt to split them, the gooey center gently sloping into a craggy break, the crumbs holding on for dear life. Follow the recipe as written and, thanks to the sour cream, you'll get a much-upgraded version of the premade sugar cookie logs you can buy from the store. Make them fancy, with sprinkles, marbling, or a dusting of cocoa powder, and they'll be pretty enough to grace any holiday party.

3½ cups **all-purpose flour**, plus more for dusting

1½ teaspoons **baking soda**

½ teaspoon **kosher salt**

1 cup (2 sticks) **unsalted butter**, at room temperature

¾ cup **granulated sugar**

1 large **egg**

½ cup **sour cream**

1 teaspoon **vanilla extract**

1 In a medium bowl, whisk together the flour, baking soda, and salt.

2 Combine the butter and sugar in a large bowl. Using a handheld mixer, beat on medium-high speed until light and fluffy, about 5 minutes. Add the egg and beat until fully incorporated. Add the sour cream and vanilla and mix until smooth. Add the flour mixture and mix on low speed until just combined.

3 Transfer the dough to a lightly floured work surface and form it into a disc. Wrap the disc in plastic wrap and refrigerate until chilled, about 1 hour.

4 Preheat the oven to 300°F. Line two baking sheets with parchment paper.

5 On a lightly floured work surface, roll out the chilled dough to ½ inch thick. Use a 3-inch round cutter to cut out circles of dough and place them on the prepared baking sheets, leaving about 1 inch between each circle.

6 Bake until the bottoms of the cookies are pale golden brown and the tops are matte, 8 to 10 minutes. Transfer the baking sheets to wire racks and let the cookies cool on the pans for 2 minutes. Using a flat metal spatula, transfer the cookies to the racks and let cool completely, about 20 minutes.

DECORATING IDEAS

1. Color half the dough with food coloring, then recombine with the plain dough and mix just enough to create a swirled, marbled effect. Roll the dough into a ¼-inch-thick sheet and cut out 3-inch cookies before baking.

2. Spread the top of each cookie with icing and, while the icing is still wet, center a small cookie cutter on each cookie, fill the inside with sprinkles, then slowly remove the cutter to reveal the sprinkles in the shape of the cutter.

3. Add drops of food coloring to a bowl of plain white icing, stir a few times to swirl the color into the icing, then dip the top of each cookie in the color swirl and let any excess drain off to reveal a tie-dye effect.

4. Center a small paper doily over each cookie and dust heavily with powdered sugar. Carefully remove the doily to reveal the sugar pattern underneath.

5. Carve the cookies into fruit shapes and decorate them with colored icing to look like the fruit (see examples at right).

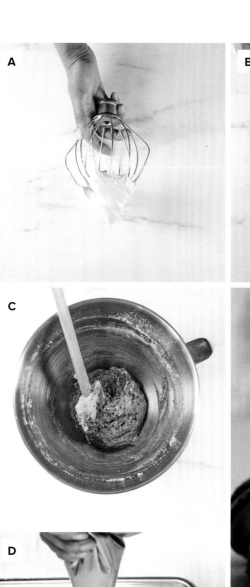

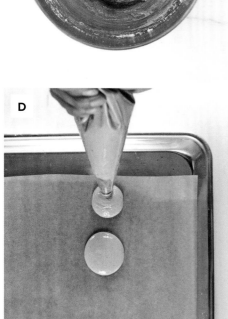

MATCHA MACARONS

Don't let their delicate appearance fool you: Beneath their crispy exterior, macarons hide an airy, chewy, and voluminous interior that nearly melts into the filling to become one big, sophisticated marshmallow. Our macaron shells, which are sandwiched with an easy cream cheese filling, get their beautiful green hue (and slightly grassy-in-good-way flavor) from matcha. And if you think macarons are hard to make, don't worry: The trickiest part is figuring out how to hold the piping bag.

SHELLS

2 large **egg whites**

½ cup **granulated sugar**

⅔ cup **confectioners' sugar**

½ cup superfine **almond flour**, such as Bob's Red Mill

2 teaspoons **matcha powder**, preferably "ceremonial grade" for best color

FILLING

2 ounces **cream cheese**, at room temperature

⅔ cup **confectioners' sugar**

1 teaspoon **whole milk**

1   Line two large baking sheets with silicone baking mats (preferably) or parchment paper.

2   Make the macaron shells: Place the egg whites in a large bowl. Using a handheld mixer, beat on medium speed until soft peaks form. While beating, slowly add the granulated sugar and beat until the whites are shiny and fluffy and form stiff peaks **A**.

3   In a medium bowl, combine the confectioners' sugar, almond flour, and matcha. Sift the matcha mixture through a fine-mesh strainer over the egg whites **B**. Fold the mixtures together with a large rubber spatula until just combined, about 60 turns **C**.

4   Transfer the matcha batter to a piping bag fitted with a ½-inch plain tip. Pipe the batter in 1½-inch-wide dollops onto the prepared baking sheets, spacing them 1 inch apart **D**. Let rest until the batter is no longer wet to the touch and a skin forms on top, 1 to 2 hours.

5   Preheat the oven to 300°F.

6   Bake until the macaron shells have risen and are dry to the touch, about 15 minutes, rotating the baking sheets from front to back and top to bottom halfway through the cooking time.

7   Meanwhile, make the filling: Combine the cream cheese, confectioners' sugar, and milk in a large bowl. Using a handheld mixer, beat on low speed until smooth, 1 minute. Transfer the filling to a piping bag fitted with a ½-inch plain tip.

8   When the macaron shells are done, transfer the baking sheets to wire racks and let the shells cool completely. Flip half the cooled macaron shells flat-side up and pipe about 1 teaspoon of the filling into the center of each. Sandwich with the remaining macarons, flat-side down, arrange on a serving plate, and serve within 1 hour, or store in an airtight container in the refrigerator for up to 2 days.

ROCKY ROAD
ICE CREAM CAKE

We're big fans of "stuff" in ice cream—cookie dough chunks, cheesecake swirls, brownie bites—which is why we're all about this DIY rocky road made by loading softened chocolate ice cream with chocolate chunks, toasted pecans, and, of course, mini marshmallows, which stay soft and chewy even as the ice cream freezes in its graham cracker crust. For additional gooey stretchiness, the finished cake is topped with even more marshmallows, which can be brûléed to achieve s'mores-level stickiness.

1 cup **graham cracker crumbs** (from 9 crackers)

2 tablespoons **granulated sugar**

1 teaspoon ground **cinnamon**

½ teaspoon **kosher salt**

4 tablespoons (½ stick) **unsalted butter**, melted and cooled

1 pint **chocolate ice cream**, softened

3 cups **mini marshmallows**

1 cup **semisweet chocolate** chunks

1 cup coarsely chopped toasted **pecans**

8 ounces **semisweet chocolate**, finely chopped

½ cup **heavy cream**

1 In a large bowl, stir together the graham cracker crumbs, sugar, cinnamon, salt, and melted butter until the crumbs are evenly moistened. Transfer the crumbs to an 8-inch springform pan and press them evenly over the bottom and ½ inch up the side of the pan. Refrigerate the crust for 30 minutes.

2 In a medium bowl, stir together the softened ice cream, 1½ cups of the marshmallows, the chocolate chunks, and pecans until combined. Scrape the ice cream mixture over the crust, cover, and freeze until set, at least 8 hours or up to overnight.

3 In a heatproof liquid measuring cup, combine the chopped chocolate and cream and microwave on high power, stirring halfway through, until the ganache is smooth and shiny. Pour the ganache over the ice cream cake and freeze until the ganache is set, about 30 minutes.

4 Sprinkle the remaining 1½ cups marshmallows over the ice cream cake. If desired, use a kitchen torch to brown the marshmallows. Serve immediately.

SNICKERDOODLES

When you think of an iconic chewy cookie—you know, the Madonna of chewy cookies—you don't think of the chocolate chip. You think of the snickerdoodle. Not only do snickerdoodles have the best cookie name ("snickerdoodle" sounds like it should be some smirking breed of dog, does it not?), but they're a timeless cookie jar staple for good reason. Peak snickerdoodles are pudgy, with cracks and ripples that you can sink your teeth into, completely confetti-bombed with cinnamon sugar, and impossible to resist.

CINNAMON SUGAR

¼ cup **granulated sugar**

2 tablespoons ground **cinnamon**

COOKIES

1 cup (2 sticks) **unsalted butter**, at room temperature

1 cup **granulated sugar**

⅓ cup packed **light brown sugar**

2 teaspoons **vanilla extract**

2 large **eggs**

2½ cups **all-purpose flour**

1 tablespoon ground **cinnamon**

2 teaspoons **cream of tartar**

1 teaspoon **baking soda**

½ teaspoon **kosher salt**

1 Preheat the oven to 325°F. Line two large baking sheets with parchment paper.

2 Make the cinnamon sugar: In a small bowl, stir together the granulated sugar and cinnamon until evenly incorporated. Set aside.

3 Make the cookies: Combine the butter, granulated sugar, brown sugar, and vanilla in a large bowl. Using a handheld mixer, beat on medium speed until pale and fluffy, about 2 minutes. Add the eggs one at a time and beat until smooth.

4 In a medium bowl, combine the flour, cinnamon, cream of tartar, baking soda, and salt. Using a fine-mesh strainer, sift the dry ingredients together over the dough. Beat on low speed until just combined.

5 Using a 1-ounce ice cream scoop or two tablespoons, portion the dough and roll into 1½-inch balls. Roll the dough balls in the cinnamon sugar, then arrange them on the prepared baking sheets about 2 inches apart.

6 Bake until the cookies are flattened and golden brown at the edges, rotating the baking sheets from front to back and top to bottom halfway through the cooking time, 15 to 18 minutes. Transfer the baking sheets to wire racks and let the cookies cool on the pans for 1 minute. Using a flat metal spatula, transfer the cookies to the racks and let cool completely. Store any remaining cookies in an airtight container in the freezer for up to 5 days.

GINGERSNAP WEDGES

What says "It's fall!" even more than pumpkin spice lattes, ornamental squashes, and crewneck sweaters? An array of spiced cakes, muffins, scones, and cookies that are warm with cinnamon, nutmeg, ginger, and cloves. Gingersnaps fit squarely into this crew, and while you might think of them as being, well, snappy, the addition of sticky molasses makes these cookies chewy and offers the bitter edge that makes them addictive. Besides, they're plenty snappy in flavor: Within those sugar-topped wedges hide bits and pieces of sharply sweet candied ginger.

1 cup plus 2 tablespoons **all-purpose flour**

½ teaspoon **baking soda**

1 teaspoon ground **ginger**

½ teaspoon **kosher salt**

¼ teaspoon ground **cinnamon**

¼ teaspoon freshly grated **nutmeg**

⅛ teaspoon ground **cloves**

½ cup packed **dark brown sugar**

3 tablespoons **unsalted butter**, melted and cooled

3 tablespoons **unsulfured molasses**

1 large **egg**, at room temperature

1 cup chopped **crystallized ginger** (5 ounces)

1 teaspoon **turbinado sugar**, such as Sugar In The Raw

1 Preheat the oven to 350°F. Line the bottom of an 8-inch round cake pan with a circle of parchment paper cut to fit.

2 In a large bowl, whisk together the flour, baking soda, ginger, salt, cinnamon, nutmeg, and cloves.

3 Combine the brown sugar, butter, molasses, and egg in a medium bowl. Using a handheld mixer, beat on medium-high speed until lightened and foamy, about 5 minutes. Add the flour mixture and beat on low speed until just combined. Add the crystallized ginger and stir with a rubber spatula until evenly incorporated.

4 Scrape the dough into the prepared pan and press it into an even layer over the bottom of the pan. Using a small paring knife, score the top of the dough into 8 wedges, then sprinkle evenly with the turbinado sugar.

5 Bake until the dough is no longer shiny and a toothpick inserted into the center comes out clean, 25 to 30 minutes. Transfer the pan to a wire rack and let the dough cool completely in the pan, about 1 hour. Invert the dough onto a cutting board, turn it right-side up, and cut along the scored lines to separate the cookie wedges before serving.

SALTED CARAMEL BROWNIES

Here's what would happen if a brownie drizzled with sticky caramel sauce suddenly Hulked. No ordinary brownies, these have a layer of melty, chewy caramel in the center *and* a coating of salt-sprinkled caramel on top. Because we want you to be able to taste (and share) these brownies ASAP, we've turned to reliably delicious caramel candies (but if you want to be a go-getter, you could certainly make your own) for the filling and the glaze. No one will complain if you want to top these with vanilla, caramel, or chocolate ice cream, too.

Nonstick cooking spray

¾ cup (1½ sticks) **unsalted butter**, melted and cooled

1 cup **granulated sugar**

½ cup packed **light brown sugar**

1 teaspoon **vanilla extract**

3 large **eggs**

1½ cups **all-purpose flour**

¼ cup **unsweetened natural cocoa powder**

1 teaspoon **kosher salt**

½ cup **semisweet chocolate chips**

1 pound 3 ounces **soft caramel candies**, such as Kraft Caramels (about 64), cut in half

¼ cup **heavy cream**

Flaky sea salt, for sprinkling

1   Preheat the oven to 350°F. Coat an 8-inch square metal baking pan with cooking spray and line the bottom and all sides with parchment paper, leaving 1 inch overhanging the sides of the pan.

2   In a large bowl, whisk together the melted butter, granulated sugar, and brown sugar. Add the vanilla and eggs and whisk until thoroughly combined.

3   In a medium bowl, combine the flour, cocoa powder, and salt. Sift the flour mixture through a fine-mesh strainer over the batter and stir until just combined. Stir in the chocolate chips.

4   Pour half the batter into the prepared pan and use a rubber spatula to spread it evenly over the bottom. Arrange half the caramel pieces in a single layer over the batter, leaving a ½-inch border on all sides. Pour the remaining batter over the caramel candies and use the spatula to gently spread the batter to cover them.

5   Bake until the brownies are matte on top and set through the center, about 35 minutes. Transfer the pan to a wire rack.

6   In a medium heatproof bowl, combine the remaining caramel pieces and the cream and microwave on high power, stirring halfway through, until the mixture is thick and smooth. Pour the caramel sauce over the brownies and smooth out the top with a rubber spatula. Sprinkle with the sea salt while warm, then let cool completely, about 2 hours.

7   Using the overhanging parchment paper as handles, lift the brownies out of the pan and set them on a cutting board. Cut into 9 squares to serve.

PEANUT BUTTER
BONANZA BARS

Get thee to the grocery store, run through the aisles, and grab any and every peanut butter–stuffed treat, from pretzels to chocolates, you can get your hands on. Sounds like your childhood fantasy, right? Chop the treats up and fold them into a batter spiked with even more peanut butter and you'll get soft gooey bars with pockets of crunch in every bite. Bake this for dessert on any random day, but especially when you're faced with a leftover Halloween bounty (we're not too old for trick-or-treating, right?).

1½ cups (3 sticks) **unsalted butter**, at room temperature, plus more for greasing

3 cups **all-purpose flour**, plus more for dusting

1 teaspoon **baking powder**

1½ teaspoons **kosher salt**

1½ cups **granulated sugar**

1 teaspoon **vanilla extract**

2 large **eggs**, at room temperature

1 cup **creamy peanut butter**, such as Skippy

½ cup **peanut butter–filled candy-coated chocolate candies**, such as M&M's (4 ounces)

½ cup **peanut butter candies**, such as Reese's Pieces (4 ounces)

½ cup coarsely chopped **peanut butter–filled pretzels** (1¾ ounces)

½ cup quartered **mini peanut butter cups**, such as Reese's (2¾ ounces)

½ cup coarsely chopped **peanut butter candy bars**, such as Butterfinger (3½ ounces)

1 Preheat the oven to 350°F. Grease a 9 by 13-inch metal baking pan with butter, line the bottom and the two long sides with a sheet of parchment paper, leaving 1 inch of paper overhanging the sides of the pan, then grease the parchment.

2 In a medium bowl, whisk together the flour, baking powder, and salt.

3 Combine the butter, sugar, and vanilla in a large bowl. Using a handheld mixer, beat on medium speed until light and fluffy, 2 to 3 minutes. Add the eggs one at a time, beating well after each addition, then add the peanut butter and beat until smooth.

4 Add the flour mixture and beat on low speed until the dough just comes together. Add the chocolate candies, peanut butter candies, pretzels, peanut butter cups, and chopped candy bars and stir with a rubber spatula until evenly combined. Transfer the dough to the prepared pan and press it into an even layer over the bottom of the pan.

5 Bake until the cake is golden brown on top and set, about 45 minutes. Transfer the pan to a wire rack and let the cake cool in the pan for 20 minutes. Using the overhanging parchment paper as handles, lift the cake out of the pan and set it on the wire rack. Remove the parchment paper and let the cake cool completely. Cut the cake into 24 squares to serve.

GOOEY EGGNOG
CAKE BARS

Finally, another way to consume your favorite holiday drink without getting so tipsy that you embarrass yourself at the holiday party. That rummy eggnog, complete with nutmeg and cloves of course, takes the form of a spiked cream cheese filling, and it meets a cakey crust to form a holiday version of gooey butter cake (the lushest, squidgiest cake around). The bottom layer is pan-crisped cake, the top is tangy cream, and the middle—where the filling meets the crust—is pure chewy magic.

Nonstick cooking spray

1 (18¼-ounce) package **yellow cake mix**

½ cup (1 stick) **unsalted butter**, melted and cooled

2 large **eggs**

1 (8-ounce) package **cream cheese**, at room temperature

4 large **egg yolks**

3 cups **confectioners' sugar**

1 tablespoon plus 1 teaspoon freshly grated **nutmeg**, plus more for garnish

½ teaspoon **kosher salt**

⅛ teaspoon ground **cloves**

1½ cups **half-and-half**

¼ cup **dark rum**

1 teaspoon **vanilla extract**

Whipped cream, for serving (optional)

1   Preheat the oven to 350°F. Coat a 9 by 13-inch metal baking pan with cooking spray, then line the bottom and the two long sides with a sheet of parchment paper, leaving 1 inch overhanging the sides of the pan, and coat the parchment with cooking spray.

2   In a medium bowl, combine the cake mix, butter, and 1 of the eggs and stir with a wooden spoon until smooth. Scrape the dough into the prepared pan and press it into an even layer over the bottom of the pan.

3   Place the cream cheese in a large bowl. Using a handheld mixer, beat on medium speed until smooth. Add the remaining 1 egg and beat until smooth. Add the egg yolks and beat until smooth. Add the confectioners' sugar, nutmeg, salt, and cloves and beat on low speed until the sugar and spices have been completely incorporated. Add the half-and-half, rum, and vanilla and beat until smooth.

4   Pour the eggnog filling over the dough in the pan and smooth out the top. Bake until the top is golden brown and the filling is just set (it will not be firm, but should not jiggle when you tap the side of the pan), 45 to 50 minutes. Transfer the pan to a wire rack and let the cake cool completely in the pan, about 2 hours.

5   Using the overhanging parchment paper as handles, lift the cake out of the pan and set it on a cutting board. Slice the cake into 2-inch squares and serve at room temperature or chilled, with a dollop of whipped cream, if you like, and a dusting of grated nutmeg.

GLUTEN-FREE
SQUIDGY COCONUT-LIME LOAF CAKE
WITH RASPBERRIES

Live, laugh, loaf! This sliceable, snackable loaf cake is mostly shredded coconut (seriously, there's 2½ cups in there!), which means that the whole thing bakes up like one big bouncy macaroon. What's even better? The layer of sweet raspberries that are hiding in the middle and the fact that, thanks to all that coconut, there's no flour necessary—gluten-free'ers, rejoice.

Nonstick cooking spray

2½ cups **unsweetened shredded coconut**

¼ cup **cornstarch**

1 tablespoon **baking powder**

1 teaspoon **kosher salt**

¾ cup canned **unsweetened coconut milk**

Finely grated zest of 2 **limes**

2 tablespoons fresh **lime juice**

1 teaspoon **vanilla extract**

¾ cup **granulated sugar**

½ cup (1 stick) **unsalted butter**, at room temperature

4 large **eggs**

1 (6-ounce) container **raspberries**, halved

2 cups **confectioners' sugar**

1 Preheat the oven to 350°F. Coat a 9 by 5-inch loaf pan with cooking spray, then line the bottom and two long sides with a sheet of parchment paper, leaving 1 inch overhanging the sides of the pan.

2 In a large bowl, whisk together the coconut, cornstarch, baking powder, and salt. In a small bowl, whisk together ½ cup of the coconut milk, half the lime zest, the lime juice, and the vanilla extract.

3 Combine the granulated sugar and butter in a separate large bowl. Using a handheld mixer, beat on medium until pale and fluffy, 3 to 5 minutes. Add the eggs one at a time, beating well after each addition, then beat until smooth. Add the shredded coconut mixture, then add the coconut milk mixture and beat on low until just combined.

4 Pour three-quarters of the batter into the prepared pan and scatter the raspberries evenly over the top. Pour the remaining batter over the raspberries and gently spread the batter to cover them completely. Bake until the cake is golden brown and a toothpick inserted into the center comes out clean, about 40 minutes. Transfer the pan to a wire rack and let the cake cool in the pan for 20 minutes.

5 Using the parchment paper as handles, lift the cake out of the pan and set it on the wire rack. Remove the parchment paper and let the cake cool completely, about 2 hours.

6 Meanwhile, in a medium bowl, combine the remaining ¼ cup coconut milk and remaining lime zest. Add the confectioners' sugar and stir until the mixture forms a thick glaze.

7 Pour or drizzle the glaze over the top of the cooled cake and let stand for 10 minutes to set the glaze before serving.

FROZEN SALTED GRAPEFRUIT

PIE BARS

These pink, pucker-inducing bars taste like a trip to the beach—if that beach is in Italy and you're holding dessert in one hand and a spritz in the other. On top of a salty, buttery cracker crust lies a bright custard filling made from reduced grapefruit juice and sweetened condensed milk. SCM (that's our pet name) not only tames the grapefruit's natural bitterness, but also allows the custard to freeze into a chewy-but-creamy layer that's like an ice cream bar, with no iciness to be found. Swath the whole thing in sweetened whipped cream so that the tangy inside is a surprise to all of your grateful friends/legion of fans.

CRUST

12 ounces **saltines**, finely crushed by hand

1 cup (2 sticks) **unsalted butter**, melted and cooled

¼ cup **granulated sugar**

½ teaspoon **kosher salt**

FILLING

3 **ruby red grapefruits**

1 cup **granulated sugar**

1 teaspoon **kosher salt**

6 large **egg yolks**

1 (14-ounce) can **sweetened condensed milk**

2 drops of **pink food coloring** (optional)

1½ cups chilled **heavy cream**

TOPPING

1½ cups chilled **heavy cream**

½ cup **confectioners' sugar**

1 teaspoon **vanilla extract**

Flaky sea salt

1   Preheat the oven to 350°F. Line the bottom and two long sides of a 9 by 13-inch metal baking pan with a sheet of parchment paper, leaving 1 inch overhanging the sides.

2   Make the crust: In a large bowl, combine the saltines, melted butter, granulated sugar, and kosher salt and toss until evenly combined. Transfer the crumbs to the prepared pan and use the bottom of a measuring cup to press them into an even layer over the bottom of the pan. Bake the crust until golden brown and set, 18 to 20 minutes. Transfer the pan to a wire rack and let the crust cool completely.

3   Make the filling: Using a Microplane, zest the grapefruits over a large bowl and set aside. Halve the grapefruits and squeeze the juice into a large measuring cup until you have 1½ cups juice. Pour the juice in a small saucepan and bring to a boil over high heat. Cook until the juice has reduced by half, 10 to 12 minutes. Pour the reduced juice into a small bowl and place in the freezer until chilled to the touch but not frozen, about 30 minutes.

4   Add the chilled reduced grapefruit juice to the bowl with the zest, then add the granulated sugar, kosher salt, egg yolks, condensed milk, and food coloring (if using). Using a handheld mixer, beat on medium-high speed until very pale, light, and foamy, about 5 minutes.

5   Pour the cream into a medium bowl. Whisk the cream until stiff peaks form. Using a rubber spatula, gently fold the

whipped cream while you slowly pour in the grapefruit custard. Pour the filling over the crust and smooth out the top with the rubber spatula. Cover and freeze until the custard is completely set, at least 4 hours or up to overnight.

6 Make the topping: Combine the cream, confectioners' sugar, and vanilla in a large bowl. Using a handheld mixer, beat on medium speed until stiff peaks form.

7 Using the overhanging parchment paper as handles, lift the bars out of the pan and set them on a cutting board. Spread or pipe the whipped cream over the top of the frozen grapefruit filling to cover it completely, then sprinkle the top with some flaky sea salt. Cut into 2-inch squares and serve while frozen.

JUICY & FRUITY

basic pie dough

**makes 2 discs for two 9-inch pies or
1 double-crust pie**

While the lattice might be the OG of
impressive pie design, there's a whole
world of pie-dough-as-artform out
there (or at least hundreds of Instagram
accounts devoted to the subject). Start
with this buttery pie dough recipe and,
with a rolling pin, a little creativity, and
some ideas from your old pals (us!),
you'll be able to make fanciful pie crusts
that are almost too pretty to cut into (but
don't be ridiculous—have a slice!).

Chilled dough is easiest to work with;
if your dough is getting melty-flabby on
you, stick it in the fridge until it's firmed
up and ready to hold its shape.

3 cups **all-purpose flour**, plus more for dusting

1 cup (2 sticks) **unsalted butter**, cut into ½-inch
cubes and chilled

1 tablespoon **granulated sugar**

2 teaspoons **kosher salt**

½ cup ice-cold **water**

1　In a food processor, combine the flour, butter,
granulated sugar, and salt and pulse until
pea-size pebbles form, about 10 pulses.
Drizzle in the water, then pulse until the
dough forms large clumps, about 10 pulses.

2　Scrape the dough onto a work surface and
press it into a ball. Cut the ball in half and
mold each half into a ½-inch-thick disc.

3　Wrap each disc separately in plastic wrap
and refrigerate for at least 1 hour and up to
2 days. (Alternatively, freeze the dough for
up to 2 months; thaw it in the refrigerator for
24 hours before using.)

DOUGH DESIGNS

(USING ONE ROLLED CRUST TO FIT A 9-INCH PIE)

1. Cut ½-inch-wide strips of dough and weave them together into a lattice pattern.

2. Cut out leaf shapes from the dough with cookie cutters, then arrange over the top of the filling. Use remaining dough to cut out thin "vines" to connect the leaves.

3. Cut out shapes from the round of dough, then place the round over the filling to show the filling peeking through.

4. Cut out shapes from the round of dough, then place them over the filling so they're floating freely on top.

5. Cut ¼-inch-wide strips of dough, weave three of them together at a time to make thicker braids, then arrange them side-by-side over the top of the pie.

6. Cut random-size swatches of dough and tile them on top of each other to create the effect of a wrapped mummy.

7. Place the round of dough over the pie. Place a round 1-inch-diameter cutter in the center of dough, then cut the dough into 16 small wedges, radiating out from the cutter to the edge of the dough. Lift each wedge, twist it lightly, then lay it back on the filling to create a sunburst pattern.

8. Cut out letters from the round of dough, then place them over the filling so they spell out a name or fun saying.

9. Place the round of dough over the pie and cut random or ordered slits in the dough all over the top of the pie.

10. Cut out 2 by 1-inch rectangles of dough and overlap them neatly to create a tiled pattern.

11. Place the round of dough over the pie. Place a round 1-inch-diameter cutter in the center of the dough, then cut the dough into 12 wedges, radiating out from the cutter to the edge of the dough. Cut the outer and inner edge of every other wedge to release it completely, then remove and discard it, leaving behind alternating wedges of covered and uncovered pie.

12. Cut out pieces of dough using a puzzle-piece cookie cutter, then connect them on top of the pie, leaving 5 to 7 pieces missing at random points over the top of the pie as if the puzzle is almost solved.

CUT-OUT

LEAVES AND VINES

LETTERS

POLKA DOT

HERRINGBONE

MUMMY

PUZZLE PIECES

PINWHEEL

SUNBURST

LATTICE

BRAID

BRICK TILE

STRAWBERRY ROSE
CREPE CAKE

serves 6 to 8

Here's what happens when you take the idea of a crepe cake—layers of round crepes spread with filling and piled high—and turn it on its side (literally). By slicing the crepes into strips, then loading them with creamy frosting and slices of strawberries before rolling them into a spiral, you'll get a giant frilly rose, with berries peeking out from between the "petals." It's stunning, sure, and each forkful guarantees a taste of strawberries and cream.

CREPES

3 cups **whole milk**

2 cups **all-purpose flour**

4 tablespoons (½ stick) **unsalted butter**, melted

3 tablespoons **granulated sugar**

3 large **eggs**

FILLING

1 (8-ounce) package **cream cheese**, at room temperature

⅓ cup **heavy cream**

3 tablespoons **granulated sugar**

5 large **strawberries**, thinly sliced

1   Make the crepes: In a large bowl, whisk together the milk, flour, melted butter, sugar, and eggs (there will be some lumps). Cover the bowl with plastic wrap and refrigerate for at least 30 minutes or up to 1 day.

2   Meanwhile, make the filling: Combine the cream cheese, heavy cream, and sugar in a medium bowl. Using a handheld mixer, beat on medium speed until smooth, about 1 minute.

3   Heat a 9½-inch nonstick skillet over medium heat. Whisk the batter again to smooth out any lumps, then pour ⅓ cup of the batter into the center of the skillet and quickly swirl it around to coat the bottom of the skillet. Cook the crepe until bubbles rise to the surface and

the bottom is golden brown, about 3 minutes. Flip and cook on the other side until the edges start to crisp slightly, about 1 minute more. Transfer the crepe to a cutting board to cool. Repeat with the remaining batter to make 16 crepes total.

4   Once cooled, stack the crepes on top of one another, then cut the stacked crepes in half. Cut each stack lengthwise in half again to make 4 strips total **A** .

5   Place two crepe strips on a cutting board, overlapping their ends by 1 inch, and spread 2 teaspoons of the filling evenly over both to glue them together **B** . Arrange strawberry slices evenly across the strip **C** . Repeat with the remaining crepe strips and filling to make about 28 strips total. Divide the remaining strawberry slices evenly among only half the crepe strips.

6   Roll up the first strip with strawberries like a cinnamon roll, then roll a plain strip around it in the same manner **D** . Repeat with the rest of the crepe strips, alternating strips with strawberries and strips without. Once it becomes too large to roll, lay the cake on its side and continue wrapping strips around the cake **E** . Loosely cover the cake, and transfer it to the refrigerator. Chill until set, at least 30 minutes or up to overnight.

7   Using a knife, slowly and gently cut the crepe cake into wedges to serve.

ORANGE SEMIFREDDO

We've already discussed our love for edible bowls once (see Ice Cream Churro Bowls, page 51), and here's another reason to join the fan club: Rather than freezing this citrusy, boozy mousse in a loaf pan or serving bowl, we chill the mixture in scooped-out orange halves. Even your most obtuse friends will be able to predict the semifreddo's flavor before they taste it, and you'll have many fewer dishes to clean. (Insert "Orange you glad you tried it?" dad joke here.)

6 **oranges**

8 ounces **mascarpone cheese**

1⅓ cups **confectioners' sugar**

2 tablespoons **orange liqueur**, such as Cointreau or Grand Marnier

2 teaspoons **vanilla extract**

3 large **egg yolks**

⅔ cup **heavy cream**

1 Halve 4 of the oranges across their equators, then juice them and remove any remaining pulp and membranes, keeping the spent shells intact. Place the 8 juiced orange halves in a muffin tin, nestling each in its own cup. Reserve the juice for another use.

2 Using a Microplane, zest the remaining 2 oranges over a large bowl (reserve the zested oranges for another use). Add the mascarpone, confectioners' sugar, orange liqueur, vanilla, and egg yolks. Using a handheld mixer, beat on medium-high speed until smooth and fluffy, about 3 minutes.

3 Pour the cream into a medium bowl. Using the handheld mixer, beat on medium speed until stiff peaks form. Gently fold the whipped cream into the orange-mascarpone mixture.

4 Fill each orange half with the filling and freeze until solid, at least 1 hour or up to 1 day. Stab a spoon into each and serve frozen.

TROPICAL KIWI
CAKE BOMBE

serves 8

Attention, fruit enthusiasts (yes, you!): There's not one, not two, but *three* fruits in this no-bake domed cake (street name: "bombe"). Rounds of ripe kiwi might decorate the outside, but the inside is filled with pieces of pineapple and orange suspended in a moussey cream. The bombe is held together by stripes of pound cake, which soak up the flavors of the fruit and cream overnight so that each piece is pudding-soft with tropical vibes. Can't you just feel the island breeze?

1 (8-ounce) package **cream cheese**, at room temperature

1 cup **confectioners' sugar**

½ teaspoon **kosher salt**

1¼ cups chilled **heavy cream**

4 or 5 ripe **kiwifruits**, peeled and sliced

1 **orange**

¼ fresh **pineapple**, peeled, cored, and finely chopped

1 (12-ounce) store-bought **pound cake**, cut into ¼-inch-thick slices

1 Combine the cream cheese, confectioners' sugar, and salt in a large bowl. Using a handheld mixer, beat on medium speed until smooth, about 1 minute. With the mixer running on low speed, slowly pour in the cream and beat until smooth, then increase the speed to medium-high and beat until stiff peaks form.

2 Line a 7-inch-diameter bowl with plastic wrap. Arrange the kiwi slices over the bottom and up the side of the bowl in a single layer, cutting them as needed to make them fit as snugly as possible. Spoon 1 cup of the whipped cream mixture into the bowl and gently spread it over the kiwi slices to cover them evenly and "cement" them in place.

3 On a cutting board, cut one end off the orange so it sits flat. Slicing along the curve of the orange, remove the peel and white pith, then cut alongside the membranes to release the segments. Coarsely chop the segments, then add them to the bowl with the remaining whipped cream mixture, leaving any juices behind. Add the pineapple and stir to combine.

4 Use half the cake slices to line the bowl over the cream and kiwi slices until completely covered, cutting the cake to fit as needed. Spoon half the fruit–whipped cream mixture into the center of the bowl and smooth out the top with a rubber spatula. Arrange a layer of pound cake slices horizontally over the fruit mixture, cutting them to fit as needed. Add the remaining fruit–whipped cream mixture and smooth out the top. Finally, add the remaining cake slices, cutting them to fit as needed (they will form the base of the bombe). Cover the bowl with plastic wrap and refrigerate until the filling is set, at least 4 hours or up to overnight.

5 Uncover the bowl and place a large serving plate upside down over the top. Invert the bowl and plate together, then remove the bowl and plastic wrap lining. Cut the cake into wedges and serve chilled.

PEACH COBBLER–STUFFED
BEIGNETS

It's not a stretch to say that the best thing you can do with store-bought pizza dough is deep-fry it. After a hot bath in the oil, that dough becomes crispy on the outside and pillowy on the inside. Sounds like a doughnut, right? In this recipe, we turn pizza dough into golden-brown fritters, each of which is a pocket for cinnamon-spiced peach filling straight out of your most summery cobbler. Don't forget the sprinkling of powdered sugar once the doughnuts come out of the fryer—use enough so that you won't be able to resist licking your fingers after polishing off a couple beignets.

2 tablespoons **unsalted butter**

1¼ cups coarsely chopped (½-inch pieces) fresh or drained canned **peaches**

⅓ cup packed **light brown sugar**

1 tablespoon **all-purpose flour**, plus more for dusting

½ teaspoon ground **cinnamon**

¼ teaspoon freshly grated **nutmeg**

2 pounds prepared **pizza dough**, thawed if frozen

1 large **egg**, beaten with 1 tablespoon **water**, for the egg wash

Vegetable oil, for frying

½ cup **confectioners' sugar**

1 Melt the butter in a large skillet over medium heat. Add the peaches and cook, stirring, until the peaches are warmed through, about 5 minutes. Add the brown sugar, flour, cinnamon, and nutmeg and cook, stirring, until the mixture thickens around the peaches, 3 to 4 minutes. Remove the skillet from the heat and let the peach mixture cool completely, about 1 hour.

2 On a lightly floured work surface, roll out the pizza dough into a 20 by 12-inch rectangle. Cut the dough into 20 rectangles. Spoon 1 tablespoon of the peach filling into the center of each rectangle, then brush the edges of the dough with the egg wash. Fold the dough rectangles in half over the filling to create a pocket and crimp the edges well to seal the filling inside. Place the beignets on a baking sheet and refrigerate while the oil heats, or cover and freeze for up to 5 days.

3 Fill a large pot with vegetable oil to a depth of 2 inches. Attach a deep-fry thermometer to the side and heat the oil over medium-high heat to 350°F. Line a baking sheet with paper towels and set it nearby.

4 Working in batches, fry 2 or 3 beignets until puffy and golden brown, 6 to 8 minutes (the cooking time is the same for chilled and frozen beignets). Transfer the beignets to the prepared baking sheet to drain briefly. Repeat to fry the remaining beignets.

5 Dust the beignets heavily with the confectioners' sugar and serve hot.

BERRIES AND CREAM
PUFF RING

When it comes to summer berries, we go a little cuckoo. These tart, juicy jewels are things of wonder, which means that when you dress them up, be it with chocolate or streusel, you want to make sure you're showing them off. This centerpiece dessert features three classics—a crisp and airy cream puff crown, a rich custard, and lots of whipped cream—all of which celebrate, rather than suffocate, our summer berry BFFs.

CUSTARD

½ cup **granulated sugar**

¼ cup **cornstarch**

2 teaspoons **vanilla extract**

4 large **egg yolks**

2 cups **whole milk**

DOUGH

½ cup (1 stick) **unsalted butter**, cut into ½-inch cubes

½ teaspoon **kosher salt**

1⅓ cups **all-purpose flour**

5 large **eggs**

ASSEMBLE

2 cups **mixed berries**, such as hulled and quartered strawberries, halved blackberries, or blueberries

2 cups chilled **heavy cream**

Confectioners' sugar, for dusting

1 Make the custard: In a medium heatproof bowl, whisk together the granulated sugar, cornstarch, vanilla, and egg yolks until they form a thick paste, then stir in the milk until smooth. Cover the bowl with plastic wrap and microwave on high power, stirring halfway through, until thickened and smooth, 3 to 4 minutes. Press the plastic wrap directly against the surface of the custard to prevent a skin from forming and refrigerate the custard until chilled and set, at least 1 hour or up to 2 days.

2 Preheat the oven to 375°F. Line a large baking sheet with parchment paper and trace a 7-inch circle in the center. Flip the parchment paper over so the circle is facing down but still visible.

3 Make the cream puff dough: In a medium saucepan, combine the butter, salt, and 1 cup water and, stirring occasionally, bring to a boil over medium-high heat. Add the flour all at once, reduce the heat to medium, and cook, stirring continuously with a wooden spoon, until the dough forms a ball and easily pulls away from the side of the pan, about 1 minute. Remove the pan from the heat and let the dough cool for 5 minutes.

(recipe continues)

4 Add 1 egg and stir until it has been fully incorporated into the dough, then add 3 more eggs, one at a time, stirring until each is incorporated before adding the next. The dough is ready when it forms a "V" shape if you lift the spoon out of the dough. Transfer the dough to a piping bag fitted with a ⅝-inch star tip.

5 In a small bowl, beat the remaining egg with 1 tablespoon water until smooth to make an egg wash. Position the prepared baking sheet in front of you. Picturing the circle as a clock and starting at 12 o'clock, pipe a ring of dough directly over the circle drawn on the parchment A . Next, starting at 4 o'clock, pipe a second ring of dough around the outside of the first ring B . Finally, starting at 8 o'clock, pipe a third ring of dough on top of the first two rings C . Brush the dough rings with the egg wash.

6 Bake for 20 minutes, then reduce the oven temperature to 350°F and bake until the cream puff ring is golden brown, puffed, and crisp, about 15 minutes more. Without opening the oven door, turn the oven off and leave the cream puff ring inside to cool completely, about 1 hour.

7 Assemble the cream puff ring: Using two flat metal spatulas, carefully transfer the cream puff ring to a cutting board. Using a serrated knife, gently split the ring horizontally like a hamburger bun, keeping the top half slightly smaller than the bottom half D . Carefully transfer the bottom half to a serving plate.

8 Transfer the chilled custard to a piping bag fitted with a ⅝-inch star tip. Pipe the custard into the hollow cavity of the bottom half E . Arrange the berries over the custard F .

9 Pour the heavy cream into a large bowl. Using a handheld mixer, beat on medium speed until stiff peaks form. Transfer the whipped cream to a clean piping bag fitted with the same ⅝-inch star tip. Pipe the whipped cream on top of the berries.

10 Place the top half of the cream puff ring over the whipped cream. Dust the top with confectioners' sugar and serve within 1 hour to keep the pastry from getting soggy.

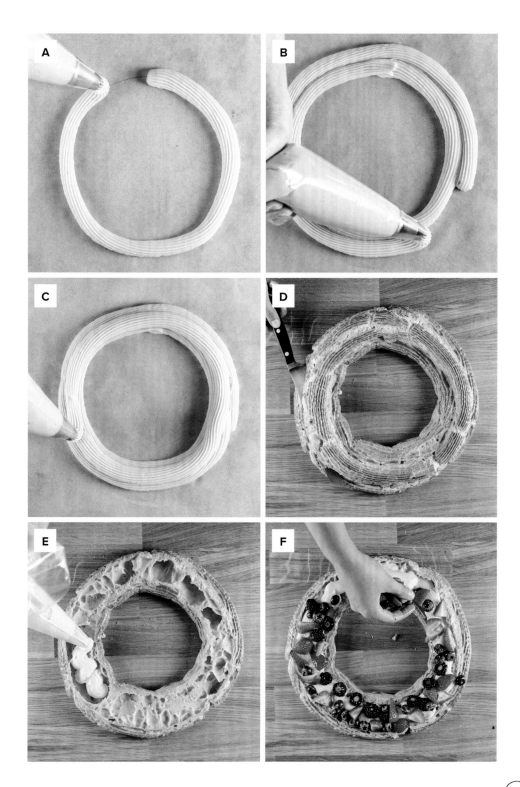

TART SUMMER BLUEBERRY PIE

With blueberries bursting from below a flaky crust, this pie is just like your great aunt's—but with one major exception: It's not overly sweet. To offset the natural sweetness of the blueberries (as well as the sugar that helps the fruit gel so that you don't have a runaway filling), we've added a lot of lemon juice and zest. The result? A pie that's pleasantly sour, tangy, and—we'll say it!—refreshing. You won't have to wash your slice down with a glass of cold water. Instead, you'll be going back for seconds.

1 recipe **Basic Pie Dough** (see page 86)

½ cup **blueberry preserves**

⅓ cup **cornstarch**

⅓ cup **granulated sugar**

Finely grated zest of 2 **lemons**

¼ cup fresh **lemon juice**

1 teaspoon **vanilla extract**

1 teaspoon **kosher salt**

2 pounds fresh or thawed frozen **blueberries** (about 6½ cups)

1 large **egg**, lightly beaten

1 tablespoon **turbinado sugar**, such as Sugar In The Raw

Whipped cream, for serving

1 Preheat the oven to 375°F.

2 On a lightly floured work surface, roll out one disc of dough into a 14-inch circle, ⅛ inch thick. Transfer the dough circle to a 9-inch deep-dish pie pan, letting it fall into the bottom and up the side.

3 Make the filling: In a large bowl, combine the preserves, cornstarch, granulated sugar, lemon zest, lemon juice, vanilla, and salt and whisk until smooth. Add the blueberries and toss until evenly coated. Scrape the blueberry filling into the pie pan and smooth out the top.

4 On a lightly floured work surface, roll out the remaining dough disc to a 12-inch circle and place it over the filling. Trim both dough circles so that ½ inch of dough hangs over the edge. Lift up the dough edge and then fold it under to form a thick crust, then press or crimp the edge to seal, as desired.

5 Brush the dough with the beaten egg, then sprinkle the turbinado sugar evenly over the top. Cut four slits in the top crust to allow steam to escape. Bake the pie until the crust is golden brown and the filling is bubbling in the center, about 1 hour 25 minutes to 1 hour 30 minutes. Transfer the pie to a wire rack and let cool completely, about 4 hours.

6 Slice the pie and garnish each with a dollop of whipped cream to serve.

SOUR CHERRY
FRITTERS

Do you have dreams about those paper bags full of hot doughnuts you can get at county fairs and old-timey roadside market stands? (It can't just be us!) In the best of those dreams, those fritters are deeply golden on the outside and airy within, filled with sweet, juicy cherries and dipped in a cherry-almond glaze. And now, with a little bit of yeast and a cherry pitter, you can make that dream a reality. If it seems annoying to fill each fritter with cherries, one by one, you're right: That's why we're showing you an easy way to get 'em all done at once.

DOUGH

¼ cup plus 1 teaspoon **granulated sugar**

2 (¼-ounce) packets **active dry yeast**

½ cup warm **water** (105° to 110°F)

¾ cup **whole milk**

⅓ cup **vegetable shortening**, plus more for greasing

1 teaspoon **kosher salt**

2 teaspoons **vanilla extract**

1 teaspoon **almond extract**

2 large **eggs**, lightly beaten

4 cups **all-purpose flour**, plus more for dusting

Vegetable oil, for greasing and frying

FILLING

1 tablespoon **unsalted butter**

3 cups fresh or thawed frozen **sour cherries**, pitted and halved (about 2½ cups)

¼ cup **granulated sugar**

1 teaspoon fresh **lemon juice**

½ teaspoon **kosher salt**

¼ teaspoon ground **cinnamon**

1 tablespoon **all-purpose flour**

GLAZE

¼ cup **cherry jam**

2 cups **confectioners' sugar**, sifted

2 tablespoons **whole milk**

1 teaspoon pure **vanilla extract**

½ teaspoon **almond extract**

1 Make the dough: In a large bowl, stir together 1 teaspoon of the granulated sugar, the yeast, and warm water and whisk to combine. Let the yeast mixture stand until foamy, about 10 minutes.

2 Meanwhile, in a small saucepan, combine the milk and shortening and heat over medium heat until the shortening has melted completely. Remove the pan from the heat and stir in the remaining ¼ cup granulated sugar and the salt until the sugar and salt have dissolved and the mixture has cooled slightly. Whisk in the vanilla, almond extract, and eggs until smooth, then pour the mixture into the bowl with the yeast mixture and whisk to combine. Add the flour and stir with a wooden spoon until the dough comes together.

(recipe continues)

3 On a lightly floured work surface, knead the dough until smooth and elastic, 8 to 10 minutes. (Alternatively, if you have a stand mixer, place the dough in the mixer bowl, attach the dough hook to the mixer, and knead the dough on medium speed for 6 to 8 minutes.) Lightly grease a large bowl with oil. Form the dough into a ball and place it in the bowl. Cover with plastic wrap and let stand until doubled in size, about 1 hour.

4 Meanwhile, make the filling: Melt the butter in a medium skillet over medium heat. Add the cherries, granulated sugar, lemon juice, salt, and cinnamon and cook, stirring, until the sugar has dissolved and no more liquid remains in the pan, 8 to 10 minutes. Sprinkle the flour over the cherries, stir to combine, and cook for 30 seconds. Remove the pan from the heat, and let the filling cool completely, about 30 minutes.

5 On a lightly floured work surface, roll out the dough to a 12 by 16-inch rectangle, ½ inch thick. Spread the cooled cherry filling over the bottom half of the dough rectangle A , then fold the other half over the top like closing a book B . Using your hands, lightly press the dough all over to remove any air pockets and adhere the cherries to the dough.

6 Cut the dough rectangle into 12 pieces C , then roll each piece in your hands D to make a rough ball with the cherries interspersed evenly in the dough E . Place the dough balls on the work surface and cover loosely with plastic wrap. Let stand until they puff slightly, about 20 minutes.

7 Fill a large Dutch oven or heavy saucepan with vegetable oil to a depth of 2 inches. Attach a deep-fry thermometer to the side and heat the oil over medium-high heat to 350°F. Line a baking sheet with paper towels and set it nearby.

8 While the oil heats, make the glaze: Place the jam in a medium heatproof bowl and microwave on high power for 10 to 20 seconds, until warm and loosened. Add the confectioners' sugar, milk, vanilla, and almond extract and stir until smooth.

9 Using a metal spatula, carefully lift 3 balls of dough and lower them into the hot oil. Fry until golden brown and cooked through, 3 to 4 minutes, turning them once halfway through the cooking time. Using a spider or slotted spoon, transfer the fritters to the prepared baking sheet to drain briefly, then transfer them to a wire rack set over a sheet of parchment paper to catch drips. Repeat to fry the remaining fritters.

10 While the fritters are hot, dip their tops in the glaze F , letting any excess drip off, then return them to the rack to cool completely and allow the glaze to set before serving, about 20 minutes. (Alternatively, drizzle the glaze evenly over the fritters.)

VANILLA-RHUBARB
SUMMER PUDDING

You wouldn't know from tasting it that the basis of summer pudding—that classic English dessert so named because it requires no baking, a boon to cooks during the hot months—is white bread. The bread doesn't have much flavor on its own, but it's so airy and absorbent that it turns spoonable and custardy by lapping up whatever sauce you soak it with. In this case, that's a sweet and sour vanilla-flecked rhubarb number, which turns the whole dessert a brilliant reddish pink.

4 cups thinly sliced **rhubarb** (12 ounces)

1¾ cups **granulated sugar**

1 cup fresh **orange juice**

1 teaspoon **kosher salt**

1 **vanilla bean**, split lengthwise and seeds scraped out

1 tablespoon fresh **lemon juice**

2 teaspoons **vanilla extract**

3 cups quartered fresh **strawberries** (14 ounces)

1 (1½-pound) **white milk bread loaf**, crust removed, cut crosswise into ½-inch-thick slices

1 cup chilled **heavy cream**, whipped to stiff peaks

1 In a large saucepan, combine the rhubarb, 1½ cups of the granulated sugar, the orange juice, salt, and vanilla bean pod and seeds and stir to combine. Bring to a simmer over medium heat, stirring often, then cook, stirring, until the sugar has dissolved and the rhubarb is tender, about 5 minutes more. Remove the pan from the heat, discard the vanilla pod, and stir in the lemon juice and vanilla extract.

2 In a large bowl, toss the strawberries with the remaining ¼ cup sugar and let stand, stirring once or twice, until the sugar has dissolved, about 10 minutes. Pour the berries and any juice collected in the bowl through a sieve or colander into a separate bowl, then pour the juice into the hot rhubarb sauce; reserve the strawberries in the sieve.

3 Line the bottom and sides of an 8-inch springform pan with plastic wrap, letting any excess hang over the edge. Spoon ¾ cup of the rhubarb sauce into the bottom of the pan and then scatter ½ cup of the strawberries over the sauce. Arrange as many slices of bread as will fit in the bottom in a pattern that you like (this will be the top of the pudding once you invert and unmold it). Pour over ¾ cup of the rhubarb sauce to saturate the bread, then scatter over another ½ cup of the strawberries. Continue layering the remaining bread slices, cutting them to fit as needed, rhubarb sauce, and strawberries. Finish with a layer of bread and any remaining rhubarb sauce (make sure to use the rest of the strawberries on the last inside layer).

4 Fold the overhanging plastic wrap over the top of the pudding, then place a 6- to 7-inch plate over the pudding. Place a couple of cans of tomatoes or a heavy cast-iron skillet on the plate to weigh it down. Refrigerate the pudding for at least 8 hours or up to overnight.

5 Remove the weight and plate from the pudding and unwrap the plastic. Invert a cake stand or serving plate over the pudding, then flip it and the pan together, letting the pudding fall onto the stand. Remove the pan and peel away the plastic wrap.

6 Spread the whipped cream on top of the pudding. Cut into wedges and serve chilled.

PLUM GALETTE
WITH WHOLE-WHEAT AND ALMOND CRUST

You know what they say: "Double the plum, double the fun." Okay, so maybe they don't say that yet, but one taste of this free-form pie and they will. It doesn't only have plums crowning the top, showing off their little yellow bellies and purple skins; it also has a thick layer of jammy plum filling hiding below. You get sour-sweet plum flavor (and purple color!) times two, plus the filling soaks up any juices the fruit gives off as it cooks so that the whole-wheat crust stays flaky and crispy.

CRUST

1 cup **whole-wheat flour**

½ cup **almond flour**

2 tablespoons packed **light brown sugar**

¼ teaspoon **kosher salt**

½ cup (1 stick) **unsalted butter**, cut into ½-inch cubes and chilled

¼ cup ice-cold **water**

All-purpose flour, for dusting

FILLING

1¼ pounds **plums**, halved, pitted, and cut into eighths

¼ cup plus 2 tablespoons **all-purpose flour**

2 tablespoons **unsalted butter**, at room temperature

2 tablespoons **granulated sugar**, plus more for sprinkling

¼ teaspoon **kosher salt**

¼ teaspoon **vanilla extract**

Pinch of ground **cinnamon**

1 large **egg**, lightly beaten

Whipped cream, for serving

1 Make the crust: In a food processor, combine the whole-wheat flour, almond flour, brown sugar, and salt and pulse to combine. Add the butter and pulse until pea-size pebbles form, about 10 pulses. Drizzle in the water, then pulse until the dough forms large clumps, about 10 pulses.

2 Scrape the dough onto a lightly floured work surface and press it into a ½-inch-thick disc. Wrap the disc in plastic wrap and refrigerate for at least 1 hour or up to 2 days. (Alternatively, freeze the dough for up to 2 months; thaw it in the refrigerator for 24 hours before using.)

3 Make the filling: In a food processor, combine ¼ pound of the plums, the all-purpose flour, butter, granulated sugar, salt, vanilla, cinnamon, and half the beaten egg and process until smooth, about 30 seconds.

4 Preheat the oven to 375°F. Line a large baking sheet with a sheet of parchment paper.

5 On a lightly floured work surface, roll out the dough to a 12-inch circle, ⅛ inch thick. Transfer the dough circle to the center of the prepared baking sheet. Spoon the filling into the center of the circle, then use an offset spatula or table knife to spread it evenly over the dough, leaving a 1½-inch border.

6 Starting from the outside edge of the filling and working toward the center, arrange the remaining 1 pound plum wedges in concentric circles, with the points of each wedge facing inward. Fold over the dough border to form a "wall" around the edge of the galette. Brush the dough with the remaining beaten egg, then sprinkle the dough and the plums with more granulated sugar.

7 Bake the galette until the crust is golden brown, the plums are caramelized on top, and the filling is bubbling in the center, about 40 minutes. Transfer the baking sheet to a wire rack and let the galette cool completely, about 1 hour.

8 Slice the galette and garnish each slice with a dollop of whipped cream to serve.

MANGO MERINGUE PIE

serves 8 to 10

CRUST

1⅓ cups **unsweetened shredded coconut**

¼ cup packed **light brown sugar**

½ teaspoon **kosher salt**

Finely grated zest of 1 **lime**

5 tablespoons **unsalted butter**, melted and cooled

FILLING

Finely grated zest of 1 **orange**

1¼ cups fresh **orange juice**, from 3 to 4 **oranges**

1 cup **granulated sugar**

1 (¼-ounce) packet **unflavored powdered gelatin**

2 ripe **mangoes**, pitted, peeled, and cut into chunks, or 2 cups thawed frozen mango chunks

1 teaspoon **kosher salt**

1 teaspoon pure **vanilla extract**

MERINGUE

½ cup **granulated sugar**

1 teaspoon **cornstarch**

1 teaspoon **cream of tartar**

½ teaspoon **kosher salt**

3 large **egg whites**, at room temperature

Will your friends be surprised when you slice into this sky-high, meringue-topped pie to reveal a custard center that's not yellow but orange? Maybe. But will they be mad? Definitely not. Switch out the classic lemon meringue for mango meringue (with a coconut-lime crust!) for a pie that tastes like a trip to the tropics no matter the time of year. And there's plenty of orange juice and zest, which'll give you the sour flavor you crave and make the mango taste even more mango-y.

1   Preheat the oven to 350°F.

2   Make the crust: In a large bowl, stir together the coconut, brown sugar, salt, and lime zest. Pour in the melted butter and stir until evenly moistened. Transfer the mixture to a 9-inch glass pie pan and press it evenly over the bottom and up the side. Bake until golden brown, about 20 minutes. Transfer the pie pan to a wire rack and let the crust cool completely, about 30 minutes.

3   Make the filling: In a small saucepan, combine the orange zest, 1 cup of the orange juice, and the granulated sugar. Bring to a boil over high heat, then reduce the heat to medium-low and simmer until slightly reduced, about 10 minutes. Remove the pan from the heat.

4   While the orange syrup cooks, pour the remaining ¼ cup orange juice into a small bowl and sprinkle the gelatin over the top. Let stand for 5 minutes to soften the gelatin, then scrape the mixture into the warm syrup and stir until the gelatin has dissolved.

5   Pour the orange mixture into a blender, add the mangoes, salt, and vanilla, and puree until very smooth. Pour the mango filling through a fine-mesh sieve into a bowl, pressing it through with a rubber spatula, then pour it into the crust. Cover the pie with plastic wrap, press it directly against the surface of the filling to prevent a skin from forming, and refrigerate the pie until the filling is set, at least 6 hours or up to overnight.

6   When you are ready to assemble the pie, make the meringue: Bring 1 inch of water to a simmer in a medium saucepan. In a large glass bowl, combine the granulated sugar, cornstarch, cream of tartar, salt, and egg whites and whisk to combine. Set the bowl over the simmering water (do not let the water touch the bottom of the bowl) and cook, whisking continuously, until the sugar has dissolved and the mixture is hot to the touch, 3 to 4 minutes. Remove the bowl from the saucepan and, using a handheld mixer, beat on medium-high speed until the meringue is light and fluffy and forms stiff peaks, about 2 minutes.

7   Spoon the meringue onto the pie, spreading it just to the edge of the filling. If desired, use a kitchen torch to lightly brown the meringue all over. Return the pie to the refrigerator to chill, at least 2 hours. Cut the pie into slices and serve cold.

CREAMY DREAMY

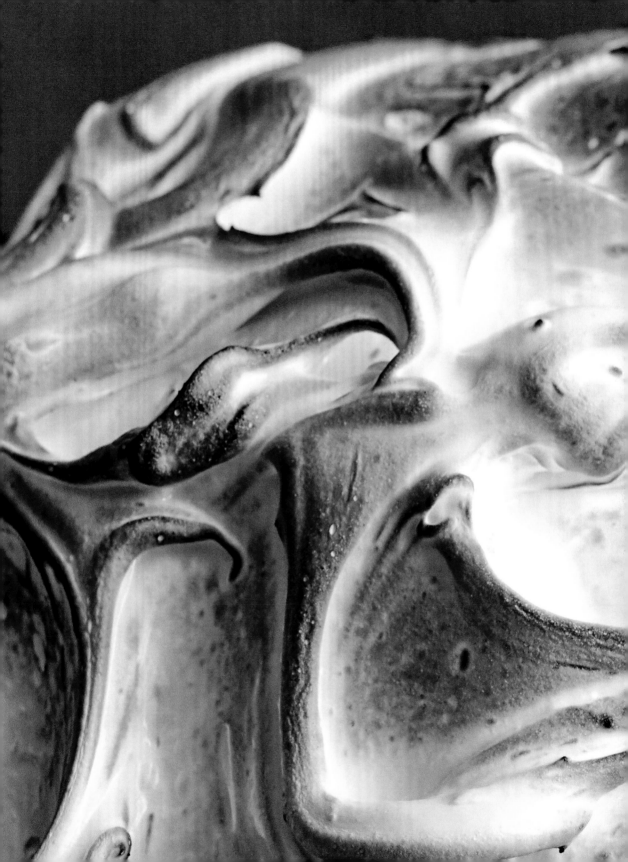

classic cheesecake

makes one 9-inch cheesecake

Think of a cheesecake as one big creamy, tangy, luscious, spoon-able canvas for all of your hopes and dreams—meaning, your favorite sauces, syrups, and smears. When you change up what goes on top based on the season (pumpkin in the fall, citrus in the winter, herbs in the spring, and berries in the summer), you'll have a rotating selection of cheese-cakes for baking and eating all year long.

12 **graham crackers**

½ cup (1 stick) **unsalted butter**, melted

3 (8-ounce) packages **cream cheese**, at room temperature

1 cup **granulated sugar**

½ teaspoon **kosher salt**

1 tablespoon **vanilla extract**

4 large **eggs**

1 Preheat the oven to 350°F. Line the bottom of a 9-inch springform pan with a round of parchment paper.

2 Add the graham crackers to the bowl of a food processor, and process to fine crumbs, about 10 seconds. Pour in the melted butter and pulse until the crumbs are evenly moistened, about 10 pulses. Scrape the crumb mixture into the prepared pan and spread it evenly over the bottom; clean the processor. Using the bottom of a dry measuring cup, press the crumbs down firmly to create an even crust. Bake the crust until lightly golden brown and set, 20 to 25 minutes. Transfer the pan to a wire rack and let stand while you make the filling. Keep the oven on.

3 Combine the cream cheese, sugar, and salt in the food processor and process, stopping to scrape the side and blade if necessary, until smooth, about 1 minute. Add the vanilla and eggs and process until smooth again, about 30 seconds.

4 Scrape the filling onto the crust and smooth the top. Return the pan to the oven and bake until light golden brown on top and the center jiggles slightly when you tap the side of the pan, 50 to 55 minutes.

5 Turn the oven off and let the cheesecake cool in the oven for 2 hours. Remove the pan from the oven and transfer it to the refrigerator to chill and set further, about 6 hours.

6 Remove the side of the springform pan, cut the cheesecake into slices, and serve cold.

SEASONAL TOPPINGS

Decorate your finished cheesecake with one of the following seasonal toppings, enough for every month of the year!

JANUARY

Citrus: Top with a mix of peeled grapefruit and orange segments.

FEBRUARY

Chocolate-Cherry: Coarsely chop chocolate-covered cherry candies and scatter them over the top.

MARCH

Mint Chip–Chocolate stripes: Alternate drizzles of melted chocolate chips and melted mint chips over the cheesecake.

APRIL

Herbs: Brush basil and tarragon leaves lightly with beaten egg white, coat in granulated sugar, and let dry to harden. Arrange the candied herbs over the cheesecake.

MAY

Flowers: Decorate the top with edible fresh blossoms or candied violets.

JUNE

Lemonade: Top the cheesecake with a generous spoonful of lemon curd.

JULY

Berries: Mix fresh blueberries and/or blackberries with a spoonful of blueberry jam, then spoon the mixture over the top.

AUGUST

Peaches: Chop fresh peaches, mix with a spoonful of peach or apricot jam, and spoon over the top.

SEPTEMBER

Apples: In a saucepan, sauté thin apple slices in butter, sugar, and cinnamon until tender, then spoon over the top while warm.

OCTOBER

Pumpkin: Warm canned pumpkin puree in a saucepan with a pat of butter, a spoonful of sugar, and a pinch each of cinnamon, nutmeg, and cloves. Spread the mixture on top while warm.

NOVEMBER

Cranberry: Spoon fresh or canned whole cranberry sauce over the top.

DECEMBER

Cookie butter: Warm cookie butter in the microwave, then drizzle over the top. Sprinkle with crushed Biscoff cookies.

JANUARY

APRIL

FEBRUARY

MAY

MARCH

JUNE

JULY

OCTOBER

NOVEMBER

AUGUST

SEPTEMBER

DECEMBER

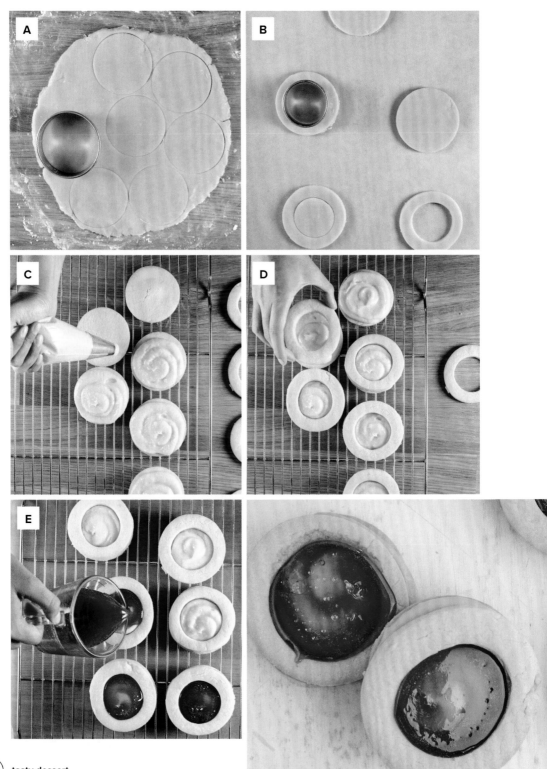

CRÈME BRÛLÉE COOKIES

There are few things on this planet more satisfying than the sharp "crack!" that comes from tapping the caramel sheet on top of crème brûlée with a spoon and watching that surface shatter into the custard below. You'll get that same pleasure here, except that the creamy pudding is nestled in caramel-covered sandwich cookies, which makes them portable, playful, and perfect for feeding a crowd.

2½ cups **granulated sugar**

3 tablespoons **cornstarch**

1 teaspoon **vanilla extract**

3 large **egg yolks**

1½ cups **whole milk**

1 cup (2 sticks) **unsalted butter**, at room temperature

2 large **eggs**

3½ cups **all-purpose flour**

1 In a large heatproof bowl, whisk together ½ cup sugar, the cornstarch, vanilla, and egg yolks until they form a thick paste. Whisk in the milk. Loosely cover the bowl with plastic wrap and microwave on high power, whisking every 1 minute, until the mixture becomes a thick custard, 4 to 6 minutes. Press plastic wrap directly against the surface of the custard to prevent a skin from forming and refrigerate until thickened, 1 to 2 hours.

2 Combine 1 cup of the sugar and the butter in a medium bowl. Using a handheld mixer, beat on medium speed until light and fluffy. Add the eggs and flour and beat on low speed until the dough just comes together. Scrape the dough onto a work surface, form it into a ball, then halve the ball. Shape each half into a disc and wrap them separately in plastic wrap. Refrigerate the discs until chilled, about 1 hour.

3 Preheat the oven to 350°F. Line two large rimmed baking sheets with parchment paper. On a lightly floured work surface, roll out 1 dough disc to ¼ inch thick. Using a 3-inch round cutter, cut out at least 6 circles of dough **A** and place them on one of the prepared baking sheets. Reroll the dough scraps and cut out at least 6 more circles, placing them on the same baking sheet. Repeat with the second dough disc, placing the circles on the second baking sheet. Using a 2-inch round cutter, cut out the centers of 12 of the circles **B** . Save the centers to bake another time or discard.

4 Bake the cookies until pale and just barely browned at the edges, about 10 minutes. Transfer the cookies to wire racks and let cool completely, about 30 minutes.

5 Transfer the chilled custard to a piping bag fitted with a ½-inch plain tip. Pipe the custard evenly onto the 12 whole cookies **C** . Place a ring-shaped cookie on top and press down gently **D** .

6 In a small saucepan, heat 1 cup sugar over medium-high heat, swirling the pan occasionally but not stirring, until the sugar turns into an amber-colored caramel. Immediately transfer the caramel to a heatproof glass measuring cup with a spout, then pour about 2 tablespoons of the caramel into the center of each cookie **E** . Let the cookies cool completely before serving.

NEAPOLITAN

BAKED ALASKA

Here's how to turn store-bought ice cream into a dessert that's a hundred times more impressive than opening up those pints and letting your guests have at it: Layer the ice cream (vanilla, strawberry, and chocolate for an old-school Neapolitan combo) into a bowl, invert the frozen dome onto a layer of cake, and enrobe the whole ice cream hill in a swoopy, billowing meringue. In every slice, you'll get soft meringue, three cold and creamy flavors of ice cream, and a foundation of cake to soak up any delicious drips.

1 pint **vanilla ice cream**, softened

2 pints **strawberry ice cream**, softened

2 pints **chocolate ice cream**, softened

1 cup **granulated sugar**

1 teaspoon **cream of tartar**

4 large **egg whites**, at room temperature

1 teaspoon **vanilla extract**

1 (9-inch) round baked and cooled **yellow cake layer** (see page 154, or from a prepared boxed cake mix)

1 Line a 9-inch bowl with plastic wrap. Scoop the vanilla ice cream into the bowl and use a rubber spatula to smooth it into an even layer. Freeze for 1 hour to firm.

2 Scoop the strawberry ice cream onto the frozen vanilla layer and use the spatula to smooth it into an even layer. Freeze for 1 hour to firm. Repeat with chocolate ice cream and freeze until ready to serve, at least 1 hour or up to 2 days.

3 Bring 1 inch of water to a simmer in a medium saucepan over medium heat. In a medium heatproof bowl, whisk together the sugar, cream of tartar, and egg whites to combine.

Set the bowl over over the simmering water (do not let the bottom of the bowl touch the water) and cook, stirring continuously, until the sugar has dissolved and the mixture is warm to the touch, 3 to 4 minutes.

4 Remove the bowl from the saucepan and add the vanilla. Using a handheld mixer, beat on medium-high speed until stiff, glossy peaks form, about 10 minutes.

5 Remove the bowl of layered ice creams from the freezer and let stand for 5 minutes at room temperature. Set the cake layer over the ice cream, then invert a cake stand or serving plate over the cake and flip the stand and ice cream bowl together. Remove the bowl and plastic wrap so the ice cream dome is resting on the cake layer.

6 Working quickly, use a rubber spatula to spread the meringue evenly over the entire cake and ice cream dome until they are fully coated, creating swirls and spikes in the meringue with the spatula. If desired, use a kitchen torch to lightly brown the peaks of the meringue all over. Cut into wedges and serve immediately, while the ice cream is solid.

COOKIES & CREAM CAKE

This might look like an ordinary, albeit tall and impressive, cake from the outside, but slice into it and you'll see that the layers are arranged vertically like zebra stripes, instead of horizontally like a traditional layer cake. Not only does this make each piece mind-boggling to gaze at, but it also means that you get more cookies and cream filling in every bite—no more picking around cake to get to the frosting. But how is this even possible? Magicians don't share their secrets, but between us: This is basically a giant roulade (a sponge cake rolled up with filling into a spiral) that's turned on its side and covered with frosting.

CAKE

1¼ cups **granulated sugar**

10 large **eggs**, separated

1 teaspoon **vanilla extract**

¾ cup **cake flour**

½ cup **unsweetened Dutch-processed cocoa powder**

½ teaspoon **baking powder**

½ teaspoon **kosher salt**

FROSTING

4½ (8-ounce) packages **cream cheese**, at room temperature

¾ cup (1½ sticks) **unsalted butter**, at room temperature

6 cups **confectioners' sugar**

1 tablespoon **vanilla extract**

24 **chocolate sandwich cookies**, such as Oreo, filling removed and cookies finely crushed, plus 5 chocolate sandwich cookies, halved, for garnish

1 Preheat the oven to 400°F. Line two large baking sheets with parchment paper.

2 Make the cake: Combine 1 cup sugar, the egg yolks, and the vanilla in a large bowl. Using a handheld mixer, beat on medium speed until pale and fluffy, about 3 minutes.

3 In a medium bowl, combine the flour, ¼ cup of the cocoa powder, the baking powder, and the salt. Sift the flour mixture through a fine-mesh sieve over the egg mixture. Fold with a rubber spatula until just combined.

4 Place the egg whites in a separate large bowl. Using the handheld mixer with clean beaters, beat on medium-high speed until soft peaks form. With the mixer running, pour in the remaining ¼ cup sugar and beat until stiff peaks form.

5 Beat one-third of the egg whites into the chocolate mixture, then gently fold in the remaining egg whites using a rubber spatula. Divide the batter between the prepared baking sheets, spreading it evenly. Bake until just firm to the touch, 10 to 12 minutes. Transfer the baking sheets to wire racks and let the cakes cool for 10 minutes.

6 Dust the tops of the cakes with the remaining ¼ cup cocoa powder. Cover each cake with parchment paper, then flip the cakes over to remove from the pans. Carefully peel away the parchment paper from the bottoms of the cakes and discard. Cut each cake in half lengthwise **A**.

7 Make the frosting: Combine the cream cheese and butter in a large bowl. Using a handheld mixer, beat on medium speed until fluffy, about 2 minutes. Add the confectioners' sugar and vanilla and beat on low speed until smooth. Stir in the crushed cookies with a rubber spatula.

8 Evenly spread 1½ cups of the frosting onto each of the 4 cake strips; set the remaining frosting aside. Starting from one short end, tightly roll one strip into a spiral. Set the end of a second cake strip against the end of the first and tightly roll the second strip around the first **B** . Repeat with the remaining cake strips **C** . Wrap the cake tightly in plastic wrap, place it spiral-side down on a cake stand or serving plate, and refrigerate until the frosting in the center is slightly firm, about 1 hour.

9 Transfer ½ cup of the frosting to a small piping bag fitted with a ½-inch plain tip or to a zip-top bag with one corner snipped off. Use the remaining frosting to cover the top and side of the cake spiral, then pipe 10 small mounds of frosting on the outer top edge of the cake. Garnish each mound with a sandwich cookie half, then refrigerate the cake to set the frosting, at least 1 hour or up to 8 hours.

10 Cut the cake into tall, thin wedges and serve chilled.

TIRAMISU

IMPOSSIBLE FLAN

The name "impossible flan"—no relation to Kim or Mission—comes from the wacky switcheroo that happens in the oven: Even though you pour the cake batter in the pan first, before covering it with custard, when you take the cake out of the oven, the flan layer will seem to have disappeared. But flip it out, and you'll see that the island of custard is perched on a pedestal of cake. How? The cake layer rises in the oven while the custard sinks, causing the two parts to trade places. Traditionally, the impossible flan (also called the chocoflan) consists of chocolate cake with caramel-vanilla custard, but here, we're turning to espresso powder, brandy, and mascarpone cheese for a tiramisu-inspired Italian twist.

CAKE

Nonstick cooking spray

1½ cups **all-purpose flour**

2 teaspoons **kosher salt**

½ teaspoon **baking soda**

½ teaspoon **baking powder**

¼ cup instant **espresso powder**

1 tablespoon **distilled white vinegar**

1 tablespoon **brandy** or **cognac**

1 teaspoon **vanilla extract**

½ cup (1 stick) **unsalted butter**, at room temperature

¾ cup **granulated sugar**

1 large **egg**

CUSTARD

8 ounces **mascarpone cheese**

1 teaspoon **vanilla extract**

1 teaspoon **kosher salt**

1 (14-ounce) can **sweetened condensed milk**

1 (12-ounce) can **evaporated milk**

4 large **eggs**

Cocoa powder, for serving

1 Preheat the oven to 375°F. Coat a 10-inch Bundt pan with cooking spray.

2 Make the cake: In a medium bowl, whisk together the flour, salt, baking soda, and baking powder. In small bowl, whisk together the espresso powder and ¾ cup warm tap water until the espresso powder has dissolved. Stir in the vinegar, brandy, and vanilla.

3 Combine the butter and sugar in a large bowl. Using a handheld mixer, beat on medium-high speed until pale and fluffy, about 4 minutes. Add the egg and beat until smooth. Add the flour mixture, followed by the coffee mixture, then beat on low speed until the batter just comes together and is smooth. Scrape the batter into the prepared pan and smooth out the top A .

4 Make the custard: In a blender, combine the mascarpone, vanilla, salt, condensed milk, evaporated milk, and eggs and blend until smooth. Flip a soup spoon over and hold it above the cake batter in the pan. Slowly pour the custard over the back of the spoon so it lands gently on the batter B .

5 Set the cake pan in the center of a large roasting pan. Pour enough very hot tap water into the roasting pan to come halfway up the

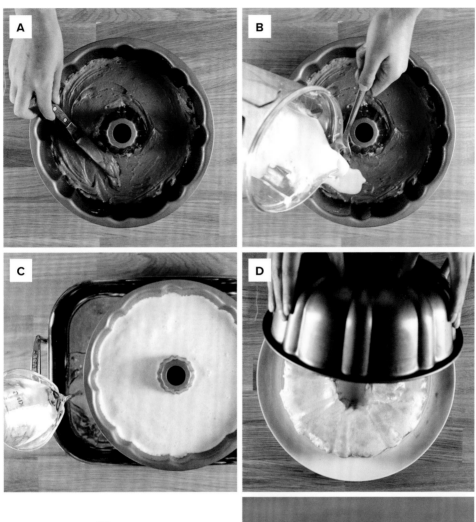

side of the cake pan C . Carefully transfer the roasting pan to the oven and bake until a toothpick inserted into the center of the cake comes out clean, 45 to 55 minutes. As the cake bakes, the custard will sink to the bottom of the pan and the cake batter will rise to the top. Remove the roasting pan from the oven, then carefully transfer the cake pan to a wire rack and let the cake cool completely, about 2 hours.

6   Invert a serving plate over the cake pan and flip them together, letting the cake and custard fall onto the plate D . Cut the cake into wedges and dust with cocoa powder.

KEY LIME

SLAB PIE

What makes this key lime pie so special? Made in a sheet pan with high sides, it can serve twice the number of people as a regular pie (or, if you're smart, the same number of people, but double the amount of servings). And yes, you'll still get the crumbly graham cracker crust, the sunny citrus custard made velvety with sweetened condensed milk, and the luscious whipped cream topping.

If you can't find key limes, which are slightly sweeter than other limes, sweeten up regular lime juice with orange juice for a good substitute.

CRUST

1¾ cups **graham cracker crumbs**

½ cup **granulated sugar**

½ cup (1 stick) **unsalted butter**, melted

FILLING

1¼ cups **sweetened condensed milk** (1½ [14-ounce] cans)

Finely grated zest of 3 **limes** (2 tablespoons)

1 cup fresh or bottled **key lime juice**, or ⅔ cup fresh regular lime juice mixed with ⅓ cup fresh orange juice

5 large **egg yolks**

WHIPPED CREAM

1½ cups chilled **heavy cream**

¼ cup **confectioners' sugar**

1 Preheat the oven to 350°F. Line the bottom and two long sides of a 9½ by 13½-inch jelly-roll pan with parchment paper.

2 Make the crust: In a medium bowl, stir together the graham cracker crumbs, granulated sugar, and melted butter until the crumbs are evenly moistened. Transfer the crumbs to the prepared pan and press them into an even layer over the bottom and up the sides of the pan. Bake until lightly browned at the edges, about 10 minutes. Transfer the pan to a wire rack and let the crust cool. Keep the oven on.

3 Make the filling: Combine the sweetened condensed milk, lime zest, lime juice, and egg yolks in a large bowl. Using a handheld mixer, beat on medium speed until pale and thickened, at least 5 minutes. Pour the filling into the crust and bake until the filling is just set in the middle, 8 to 10 minutes. Transfer the pan to a wire rack and let the pie cool completely, about 1 hour. Refrigerate the pie for at least 4 hours or up to overnight to firm up further.

4 Make the whipped cream: Combine the cream and confectioners' sugar in a medium bowl. Using a handheld mixer, beat on medium speed until stiff peaks form. Scrape the whipped cream into a piping bag fitted with a ½-inch star tip or a zip-top plastic bag with one corner snipped off.

5 Cut the pie in half crosswise, then cut each half crosswise on an angle every 1½ inches to make 16 long, thin wedges. Pipe the whipped cream evenly over each wedge and serve chilled.

LEMON BAVARIAN
LAYER CAKE

Raise your hand if you eat layer cakes primarily for the frosting. The only problem with stacking a cake to the ceiling with buckets of filling is when it oozes and runs, causing the layers to lean, Tower of Pisa style. The solution is to use Bavarian cream, an egg custard that's set with gelatin (stable enough to support the cakes!) and lightened with whipped cream (to make it more moussey than jiggly). Each layer of lemon-scented cake is tucked into a springform pan, loaded with lemon Bavarian cream, and set in the fridge until you have a citrusy and fresh eight-layer skyscraper, with as just as much luscious filling as cake.

CAKE LAYERS

1 cup (2 sticks) **unsalted butter**, at room temperature, plus more for greasing

2½ cups **cake flour**, plus more for dusting

1 teaspoon **baking soda**

1 teaspoon **kosher salt**

1 cup **buttermilk**

1 tablespoon **vanilla extract**

2 cups **granulated sugar**

Finely grated zest of 2 **lemons**

5 large **eggs**

BAVARIAN CREAM

¼ cup **unflavored powdered gelatin**

3 cups **granulated sugar**

1 tablespoon **kosher salt**

16 large **egg yolks**

3 cups fresh **lemon juice**, from 12 to 16 lemons

3 cups chilled **heavy cream**

1. Preheat the oven to 350°F. Grease two 8-inch round cake pans with butter, line the bottom of each with a round of parchment paper cut to fit, and grease the parchment. Dust the pans with flour to coat and tap out any excess.

2. Make the cake: In a medium bowl, whisk together the flour, baking soda, and salt. In a small bowl, whisk together the buttermilk and vanilla.

3. Combine the butter, sugar, and lemon zest in a large bowl. Using a handheld mixer, beat on medium-high speed until pale and fluffy, 3 to 5 minutes. Add the eggs one at a time, beating well after each addition before adding the next, then beat until smooth.

4. Add one-third of the flour mixture, followed by half the buttermilk mixture, and beat on low speed until almost combined. Repeat with half the remaining flour mixture and the remaining buttermilk mixture. Add the remaining flour mixture and beat until just combined and smooth. Divide the batter between the prepared pans and smooth out the tops with a rubber spatula.

(recipe continues)

5 Bake the cakes until a toothpick inserted into the center of each comes out clean, 30 to 40 minutes. Transfer the pans to a wire rack and let the cakes cool in the pans for 20 minutes. Invert the cakes onto the rack, remove the pans and parchment rounds, and let cool completely, about 1 hour. Using a serrated knife, trim the tops of the cakes so they're level, then halve each cake horizontally to make 4 cake layers total.

6 Make the Bavarian cream: Pour 1 cup water into a small bowl and sprinkle the gelatin over the top. Stir to combine, then let stand for 5 minutes to soften the gelatin.

7 In a medium saucepan, whisk together the sugar, salt, and egg yolks into a smooth paste. Add the lemon juice and 1¼ cups water and whisk until smooth. Place the pan over medium heat and cook, stirring continuously with a wooden spoon, until the mixture thickens enough to coat the back of the spoon, about 20 minutes.

8 Remove the pan from the heat, then immediately pour in the gelatin mixture and stir until the gelatin has dissolved. Pour the custard through a fine-mesh strainer into a large bowl, pressing it through with a rubber spatula, and let cool to room temperature, stirring occasionally, about 1 hour.

9 When the custard has cooled to room temperature, pour the heavy cream into a large bowl. Using a handheld mixer, beat on medium-high speed until stiff peaks form. While stirring with a large whisk, slowly pour the custard into the whipped cream until completely smooth.

10 Wrap the entire outside of a 9-inch springform pan in foil. Place the pan on a large rimmed baking sheet. Cut a 30-inch-long sheet of parchment paper, then fold it in half lengthwise to make an at least 7½-inch-wide, double-thick strip. Place the parchment strip, open side facing down, against the inside of the springform ring. Use a small piece of tape to secure the end of the parchment, then remove the parchment ring from the pan and tape the entire seam, inside and outside, to seal it **A** . Return the parchment ring to the pan (this makes the pan taller) **B** .

11 Place one cake layer in the bottom of the parchment ring, centering it so there's equal space between the cake and the parchment all the way around. Pour 3 cups of the Bavarian cream over the cake **C** and spread it around so it fills the gap between the cake and the parchment ring and forms a smooth layer over the cake. Place the cake pan in the refrigerator and chill to set the Bavarian cream layer, 1 hour.

12 Remove the cake pan from the refrigerator, place another cake layer over the Bavarian cream layer **D** , centering it again, and pour over another 3 cups of the Bavarian cream **E** , smoothing out the top. Refrigerate for another 1 hour, then repeat the whole process twice more with the remaining 2 cake layers and the remaining 6 cups Bavarian cream. Once the last layer of Bavarian cream is used, transfer the cake pan to the refrigerator and chill until the Bavarian cream is completely set, at least 4 hours or up to overnight.

13 Just before serving, remove the cake pan from the refrigerator. Remove the foil and the outer ring of the springform pan **F** . Peel away the parchment ring **G** . Cut the cake into wedges and serve chilled.

HONG KONG–STYLE
EGG CUSTARD TARTS

There are egg custard tarts the world over, from Portugal to England to—*ding, ding, ding*—Hong Kong, and now they can be from your kitchen, too. Each tart is adorably palm-sized, with an egg-yolk-rich custard center cradled in a flaky crust, and the process requires no special molds or equipment: Just press the pastry dough into a muffin tin, then fill each cup with the bright yellow custard and bake. In Hong Kong, egg custard tarts are served as part of a dim sum feast—which means that, yes, you should eat them for breakfast.

PASTRY

1½ cups **cake flour**, plus more for dusting

½ cup **confectioners' sugar**

½ teaspoon **kosher salt**

½ cup (1 stick) **unsalted butter**, at room temperature

2 large **egg yolks**

FILLING

6 tablespoons **granulated sugar**

½ teaspoon **kosher salt**

¼ cup **evaporated milk**

¼ teaspoon **vanilla extract**

2 large **egg yolks**

Nonstick cooking spray

1 Make the pastry: In a large bowl, whisk together the flour, confectioners' sugar, and salt. Add the butter and mix with your fingers until the mixture forms pea-size crumbles. Add the egg yolks and 1 tablespoon cold water and mix until the dough is moistened and starts to hold together. Cover the bowl with plastic wrap and refrigerate the dough for 30 minutes.

2 Make the custard filling: In a medium bowl, whisk together the sugar, salt, and ¾ cup hot tap water until the sugar has dissolved and the syrup is cool to the touch. Stir in the evaporated milk, vanilla, and egg yolks until smooth, then pour the custard through a fine-mesh strainer into a liquid measuring cup, pressing it through with a rubber spatula. Cover and refrigerate the custard until chilled, about 30 minutes.

3 Preheat the oven to 400°F. Coat a 12-cup muffin tin with cooking spray.

4 Divide the dough into 12 equal portions and roll each into a ball. Place each ball in one cup of the prepared muffin tin and press it evenly over the bottom and ½ inch up the side of the cup to create a tart shell.

5 Divide the custard filling evenly among the tart shells. Bake until the surface of the custard is golden brown and a toothpick inserted into the center stands upright, about 15 minutes.

6 Transfer the pan to a wire rack and let the egg tarts cool to room temperature, about 30 minutes. Remove the tarts from the muffin tin to serve.

BUTTERSCOTCH PUDDING

WITH CARAMEL AND SEA SALT

White sugar is to caramel what brown sugar is to butterscotch: Both are made from cooked sugar, but butterscotch has a sweeter, even richer quality. To turn butterscotch into pudding, brown sugar gets cooked with egg yolks, milk, cream, cornstarch, butter, and—while the "scotch" part of butterscotch doesn't refer to scotch or Scotland—a dash of dark rum, for added complexity. Since butterscotch pudding can be a lot to handle on its own, we're striping it with subtler vanilla pudding and bolder caramel pudding for a dessert that never gets tiresome. But don't skip the finishing touch: It's the sprinkle of salt that brings out all of the deep, molasses-y flavors and prevents the pudding from being mono-sweet.

BUTTERSCOTCH PUDDING

¼ cup plus 2 tablespoons packed **dark brown sugar**

2 tablespoons **cornstarch**

½ teaspoon **kosher salt**

2 large **egg yolks**

1 cup **whole milk**

¾ cup **heavy cream**

2 tablespoons **unsalted butter**, cut into 4 pieces

2 teaspoons **dark rum**

1 teaspoon **vanilla extract**

CARAMEL AND VANILLA PUDDINGS

1 cup **granulated sugar**

¼ cup **heavy cream**, at room temperature

¼ cup **cornstarch**

½ teaspoon **kosher salt**

6 large **egg yolks**

3½ cups **whole milk**

2 tablespoons **unsalted butter**, cut into 4 pieces

1 tablespoon **vanilla extract**

Flaky **sea salt**, for serving

1 Make the butterscotch pudding: In a medium saucepan, whisk together the brown sugar, cornstarch, and kosher salt. Add the egg yolks and stir until the mixture forms a thick paste. Pour in the milk and cream and whisk until smooth. Set the pan over medium heat and cook, stirring steadily with the whisk, until the pudding is thickened and bubbles begin to break the surface, about 6 minutes. Remove the pan from the heat and whisk in the butter, rum, and vanilla until the butter has melted and the mixture is smooth.

2 Set eight 8-ounce rocks glasses or other short cocktail glasses or mason jars on a rimmed baking sheet. Divide the pudding among the glasses and smooth out the tops. Refrigerate the butterscotch puddings on the baking sheet while you continue to work.

3 Make the caramel and vanilla puddings: Rinse out the saucepan you used for the butterscotch pudding and wipe it dry. Place ¼ cup granulated sugar in the clean saucepan and heat over medium heat, stirring occasionally with a rubber spatula or wooden spoon, until the sugar liquefies and turns into a dark amber caramel, about

5 minutes. Remove the pan from the heat and pour in the cream (it will bubble up violently). Stir until smooth and well combined. Pour the caramel sauce into a small bowl and let cool. Rinse out the saucepan and wipe it dry.

4   In the cleaned saucepan, whisk together the remaining ¾ cup sugar, the cornstarch, and the kosher salt. Add the egg yolks and stir until the mixture forms a thick paste. Pour in the milk and whisk until smooth. Set the pan over medium heat and cook, stirring steadily with the whisk, until the pudding is thickened and bubbles begin to break the surface, 8 to 10 minutes.

5   Remove the pan from the heat and whisk in the butter and vanilla until the butter has melted and the mixture is smooth.

6   Remove the baking sheet with the butterscotch puddings from the refrigerator. Gently pour half the vanilla pudding over the butterscotch pudding in the glasses and smooth out the tops. Refrigerate the puddings for 20 minutes.

7   Add the cooled caramel sauce to the remaining vanilla pudding in the saucepan and whisk to combine. Remove the baking sheet from the refrigerator. Gently pour the caramel pudding over the vanilla pudding in the glasses and smooth out the tops. Cover and refrigerate the puddings until completely set, at least 2 hours or up to overnight.

8   Sprinkle the top of each pudding with some flaky salt and serve chilled.

SESAME SWIRL ICE CREAM
WITH TAHINI CARAMEL SAUCE

serves 8

Sesame seeds are adored in cuisines 'round the world, and for good reason. In Japan, black sesame lends an earthy, roasted flavor to mile-high soft serve that's the color of wet cement but the flavor of heaven itself. In the Middle East, white sesame paste (aka tahini) is crystallized into the crumbly candy called halva. And we're finally getting up to speed in the US of A, where tahini's being swirled into brownies and black sesame paste is getting rolled into morning buns. Here, we're calling on both black and white sesame seeds to make two no-churn ice creams that get whirled together in a galactic pan of ice cream. And because we can never have too much sesame, we're topping the scoops with caramel that's boosted with tahini at the very end. It makes the sauce creamier, thicker, and a little less sweet—in other words, more sophisticated.

¼ cup plus 1 teaspoon **white sesame seeds**, plus more for garnish, if desired

¼ cup plus 1 teaspoon **black sesame seeds**, plus more for garnish, if desired

2 cups chilled **heavy cream**, plus ¼ cup, at room temperature

1 (14-ounce) can **sweetened condensed milk**

1 cup **granulated sugar**

½ cup (1 stick) **unsalted butter**

½ cup **tahini** or peanut butter

1 teaspoon **kosher salt**

1 teaspoon **vanilla extract**

1   Heat a small dry skillet over medium-high heat for 2 minutes. Add the white sesame seeds and cook, swirling the skillet occasionally, until lightly browned and toasted, 1 to 2 minutes. Transfer 1 teaspoon of the seeds to a small bowl and immediately pour the remaining hot sesame seeds into a spice grinder, coffee grinder, mortar, or small food processor. Grind or process until coarsely ground. Transfer the ground white sesame seeds to a separate small bowl and let cool.

2   Heat the same small skillet over medium-high heat for 2 minutes. Add the black sesame seeds and cook, swirling the skillet occasionally, until fragrant and toasted, 1 to 2 minutes. Transfer 1 teaspoon of the black sesame seeds to the bowl with the whole white sesame seeds and immediately pour the remaining hot black sesame seeds into a spice grinder, coffee grinder, mortar, or small food processor. Grind or process until coarsely ground. Transfer the ground black sesame seeds to a separate small bowl and let cool.

3   Combine the 2 cups chilled heavy cream and the condensed milk in a large bowl. Using a handheld mixer, beat on medium-high speed until stiff peaks form, 10 to 12 minutes. Spoon half the whipped cream into a medium bowl and fold in the ground white sesame seeds until evenly combined. Add the ground black sesame seeds to the other bowl of whipped cream and fold until evenly combined.

4   Alternately spoon the black and white sesame mixtures into a 9 by 5-inch loaf pan to create a mottled effect. Sprinkle the top with the mixed whole black and white sesame seeds, then freeze until solid, at least 4 hours or up to 24 hours.

5   Meanwhile, in a medium saucepan, heat the sugar over medium-high heat, stirring occasionally with a rubber spatula or wooden spoon, until the sugar liquefies and turns into a dark amber caramel, 6 to 8 minutes.

Remove the pan from the heat and stir in the butter and ¼ cup room temperature cream until the butter has melted and the mixture is smooth. Add the tahini, salt, and vanilla and stir until smooth. Pour the tahini-caramel sauce into a small bowl and let cool completely, about 4 hours.

6   To serve, scoop the ice cream into bowls and drizzle with the tahini-caramel sauce. Sprinkle with more toasted sesame seeds, if you like.

SOFT & FLUFFY

basic birthday cake frosting

makes 4 cups

Your birthday is the one and only day of the year when you get to do exactly what you want to (within reason, people). And that means that if you don't want classic yellow cake with chocolate frosting, you don't have to have it. Here are our ideas for making your frosting as special as you are, you little snowflake, you.

10 cups **confectioners' sugar**, sifted
1 teaspoon **kosher salt**
1 cup (2 sticks) **unsalted butter**, at room temperature
¼ to ½ cup **whole milk**
1 tablespoon **vanilla extract**

Whisk together the confectioners' sugar and salt in a large bowl. Add the butter and, using a handheld mixer, beat on low speed until the sugar has been incorporated and the frosting is very thick. Add ¼ cup milk and the vanilla and beat on low speed, gradually increasing to medium-high, until fluffy, adding more milk, if necessary, to achieve a spreadable consistency.

FROSTING FLAVORS

1. **VANILLA:** Add the seeds of **1 vanilla bean** (split lengthwise and scraped out with the tip of a knife) to the frosting when you add the butter.

2. **MALTED CHOCOLATE:** Whisk ¼ cup Dutch-processed **cocoa powder** and 2 tablespoons **malted milk powder** into the confectioners' sugar before mixing the frosting.

3. **CONFETTI:** Stir 1 cup **multicolored sprinkles** into the frosting at the end.

4. **CREAM CHEESE:** Reduce the butter to ¼ cup (½ stick) and add one 8-ounce package **cream cheese** to the frosting with the butter.

5. **CARAMEL SWIRL:** Pour 1 cup prepared **caramel sauce** into the frosting and fold until it is lightly swirled into the frosting.

6. **RED BERRIES:** Mix 1 cup whole **raspberries** and ½ cup finely chopped **strawberries** with ½ cup **raspberry jam** until evenly combined. Add to the frosting and fold until the berries are lightly swirled into the frosting.

7. **CITRUS:** Add the finely grated zest of **1 orange**, **1 lemon**, or **2 limes** when you add the butter. Substitute 6 tablespoons of the milk with 6 tablespoons of fresh **orange juice**, **lemon juice**, or **lime juice**. After mixing, stir in 2 or 3 drops of **orange**, **yellow**, or **green food coloring**, if you like.

8. **PEANUT BUTTER CRUNCH:** Add ¾ cup **smooth peanut butter** when you add the milk, adding a couple tablespoons more milk, if needed, to thin out the frosting until spreadable. After mixing, stir in 1 cup chopped honey-roasted or plain toasted **peanuts**.

CARROT CAKE

Forget what you *think* you know about vegan cakes. This three-tiered beauty is as soft and fluffy as cakes come, thanks to an all-star team of vegan ingredients. Soaked cashews turn into a sweet, spreadable frosting when blended with coconut cream and maple syrup. And the cake itself, even though it's made with whole-wheat flour and brimming with carrots, raisins, and walnuts, is tender and light because of applesauce and almond milk.

FROSTING

2⅔ cups raw **cashews**

Boiling **water**

⅔ cup **confectioners' sugar**

½ cup refined **coconut oil**, melted

⅓ cup **maple syrup**

¼ cup canned **coconut cream**

2 tablespoons fresh **lemon juice**

2 teaspoons **vanilla extract**

1 teaspoon **cider vinegar**

1 teaspoon **kosher salt**

CAKES

Nonstick cooking spray made with coconut oil

All-purpose flour, for dusting

3½ cups **whole-wheat flour**

1 cup packed **light brown sugar**

1½ tablespoons **baking powder**

1 tablespoon **baking soda**

1 tablespoon ground **cinnamon**

2 teaspoons freshly grated **nutmeg**

1 teaspoon **kosher salt**

3 cups unsweetened **almond milk**

1 cup unsweetened **applesauce**

¾ cup refined **coconut oil**, melted

¾ cup **maple syrup**

1 tablespoon **vanilla extract**

1 tablespoon **cider vinegar**

2 cups finely grated **carrots**

½ cup **raisins**

½ cup finely chopped **walnuts**

1 **carrot**, for garnish

1. Place the cashews in a large bowl and pour over enough boiling water to cover them. Let the cashews soak for at least 1 hour. Drain and rinse the cashews.

2. In a food processor or blender, combine the cashews, confectioners' sugar, melted coconut oil, maple syrup, coconut cream, lemon juice, vanilla, vinegar, and salt. Process, scraping down the sides as necessary, until completely smooth. Scrape the frosting into a bowl and place in the freezer while you make the cakes.

3. Preheat the oven to 350°F. Spray three 8-inch round cake pans with cooking spray, line the bottoms with rounds of parchment paper cut to fit, and spray the parchment. Dust the pans with flour to coat and tap out any excess.

4. Make the cakes: In a large bowl, whisk together the flour, brown sugar, baking powder, baking soda, cinnamon, nutmeg, and salt. In a separate large bowl, whisk together the almond milk, applesauce, melted coconut oil, maple syrup, vanilla, and vinegar. Pour the milk mixture over the flour mixture and whisk until just combined. Stir in the grated carrots and raisins.

5. Divide the batter evenly among the three prepared pans and smooth out the tops with a rubber spatula. Bake until a toothpick inserted into the center of each cake comes out clean, about 35 minutes. Transfer the pans to wire racks and let the cakes cool completely, about 1 hour. Invert the cakes onto the racks and remove the pans and parchment paper.

6. Remove the cashew frosting from the freezer and stir it until smooth and spreadable. Place one cake layer on a cake stand or serving plate and top with one-third of the frosting, spreading it evenly over the surface. Top with the second cake layer and frost it with half the remaining frosting. Set the final cake layer on top and frost the top of the cake with the remaining frosting, leaving the sides bare.

7. Sprinkle the top of the cake with the walnuts, then, if you like, use a Microplane to grate some fine shavings of carrot over the cake. Refrigerate the cake until set, at least 1 hour or up to 1 day. Serve chilled.

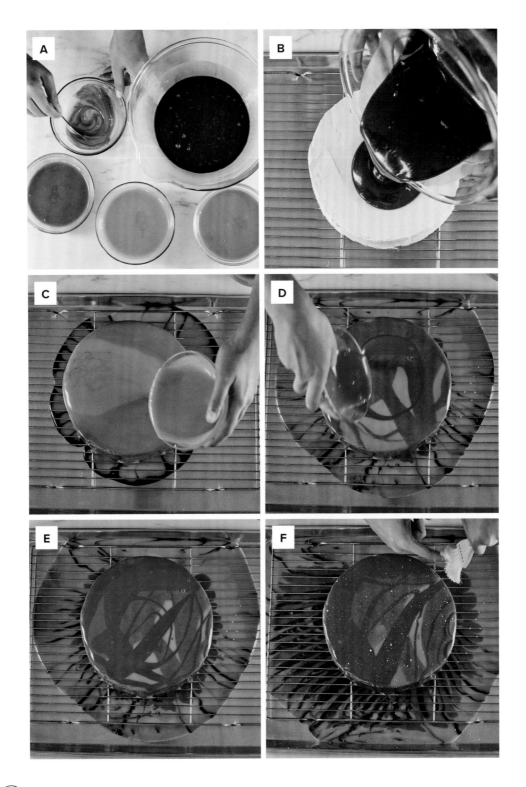

GALAXY

GALAXY
MIRROR-GLAZED CAKE

This cake has all of the mystery, intrigue, and otherworldliness of a crystal ball, only in edible form. The glassy surface is made from a mixture of white chocolate, sweetened condensed milk, and sugar that's set with gelatin so that it sticks to (rather than falls off) the cake. The Milky Way effect looks like the work of an artiste but is quite simple: Divvy up that glaze, give each portion a different hue, then pour the colors over the cake and watch them swirl together into a night sky. (Tell us this doesn't make you feel like Van Gogh.) Gaze into the finished cake and you'll feel like there's some bigger force out there in the great beyond. And, it just so happens, that bigger force is the two layers of chocolate cake, covered in vanilla buttercream.

VANILLA BUTTERCREAM & CAKE

6 cups **confectioners' sugar**

2 cups (4 sticks) **unsalted butter**, at room temperature

2 teaspoons **vanilla extract**

1 tablespoon **whole milk**

2 (9-inch) round baked and cooled **chocolate cakes** (see page 154, or prepared boxed cakes)

GALAXY MIRROR GLAZE

1 pound 10 ounces **white chocolate**, finely chopped

1½ cups **granulated sugar**

1 (14-ounce) can sweetened **condensed milk**

15 sheets of **gelatin**, silver or gold grade

Black, navy blue, light blue, purple, pink, and white **gel food coloring**

1 Make the vanilla buttercream: Combine the confectioners' sugar, butter, vanilla, and milk in a large bowl. Using a handheld mixer, beat on medium speed until smooth and fluffy, about 3 minutes.

2 Trim the tops of both cakes so they're level. Place one cake on a 9-inch cardboard cake circle on a cake stand. Top the cake with

1½ cups of the buttercream, spreading it evenly over the surface. Place the second cake over the buttercream, then frost the entire cake with the remaining buttercream, making sure to create a smooth surface on the top and side. Freeze the cake until ready to glaze, up to 2 hours.

3 Make the glaze: Place the white chocolate in a heatproof bowl.

4 In a medium saucepan, combine the granulated sugar, condensed milk, and 1¼ cups water and bring to a boil over high heat. Boil for 1 minute, then remove from the heat.

5 Fill a large bowl with 8 cups water. Place the gelatin in the water and let stand for 5 minutes to soften, then squeeze the gelatin sheets to remove excess water and stir them into the warm milk syrup until smooth. Pour the syrup over the chocolate and let sit, undisturbed, for 3 minutes. Using an immersion blender, blend the chocolate and syrup together until super smooth and shiny. Pour the glaze through a fine-mesh strainer into a separate large bowl to remove any excess bubbles.

6 Pour half the glaze into a medium bowl, then separate the remaining glaze among four

(recipe continues)

smaller bowls (exact measurements aren't important). Color the biggest bowl of glaze with black and navy blue food coloring, stirring to distribute the color evenly. Color one small bowl of glaze navy blue, another light blue, another purple, and another pink A .

7 Place the cake, still on the cardboard circle, on a wire rack set over a rimmed baking sheet to catch any excess glaze. While the glazes are still warm to the touch, carefully pour the black-and-blue glaze over the cake B , followed quickly by drizzling the navy blue glaze, then the light blue glaze C , then the

purple glaze, and finally the pink glaze D . Let the glazes blend and flow together over the side of the cake and onto the baking sheet below E .

8 Dip a pastry brush into some white food coloring, then use your fingers to spray it onto the cake to create stars F . Let the cake stand for 10 minutes to allow the glaze to set lightly. Use a paring knife to trim any drips around the bottom edge of the cake, then transfer the cake back to the cake stand. Refrigerate the cake for at least 30 minutes or up to 8 hours to set the glaze before serving.

SUPER-SOFT
BANANA BREAD COOKIES

Hi, lovers of soft, fluffy cookies! We have something for you: These cakey rounds, each of which is like a slice of your favorite banana bread, chocolate chips and all. Extra tender from Greek yogurt, these "cookies" can pass as breakfast, but they also stay soft and chewable even when they're frozen, which means they are perfect to use for ice cream sandwiches. Try pressing two together with a scoop of chocolate, coffee, or cinnamon ice cream in between and, if you can, let them re-freeze before digging in.

2 cups **all-purpose flour**

2 teaspoons ground **cinnamon**

½ teaspoon **baking powder**

½ teaspoon **baking soda**

½ teaspoon **kosher salt**

½ cup (1 stick) **unsalted butter**, at room temperature

½ cup **granulated sugar**

¼ cup packed **light brown sugar**

1 teaspoon **vanilla extract**

¾ cup mashed **bananas** (about 2 medium)

½ cup **plain Greek yogurt**

1 large **egg**

½ cup **mini bittersweet** or **semisweet chocolate chips**

1 Preheat the oven to 350°F. Line two large baking sheets with parchment paper.

2 In a medium bowl, whisk together the flour, cinnamon, baking powder, baking soda, and salt.

3 In a large bowl, whisk together the butter, granulated sugar, brown sugar, and vanilla until creamy and smooth. Add the bananas, yogurt, and egg and mix thoroughly. Add the flour mixture and the chocolate chips and gently fold in until just combined.

4 Using a 2-ounce ice cream scoop or two tablespoons, drop spoonfuls of the dough onto the prepared baking sheets, spacing them evenly apart. Bake until the cookies are light golden brown and set at the edges, 18 to 20 minutes.

5 Transfer the baking sheets to wire racks and let the cookies cool completely on the pans before serving. Store any remaining cookies in an airtight container in the freezer for up to 5 days.

BANOFFEE PIE
DOUGHNUTS

makes 12 doughnuts

Of all the portmanteaus in the dictionary—brunch, liger, turducken, gerrymander—banoffee has got to be among our favorites. A combination of *banana* and *toffee* (nope, not coffee), the English banoffee pie typically consists of the aforementioned ingredients layered in a cookie crust and mounded with whipped cream. But since we can't resist a doughnut fresh from the fryer, we translated the banoffee ingredients into doughnut form. The yeasted dough is itself banana flavored, and, once fried, it's filled with banana toffee sauce, dipped in milky glaze, and coated in crushed cookies. Should we call them "banoffeenuts"? (Don't answer that . . .)

DOUGH

¼ cup plus 1 teaspoon **granulated sugar**

2 (¼-ounce) packets **active dry yeast**

¼ cup **whole milk**, warmed to 105° to 110°F

¾ cup smooth-mashed very ripe **bananas** (about 2 medium)

4 tablespoons (½ stick) **unsalted butter**, melted, plus more for greasing

1 teaspoon **kosher salt**

1 teaspoon **vanilla extract**

2 large **eggs**, lightly beaten

4 cups **all-purpose flour**, plus more for dusting

FILLING

½ cup (1 stick) **unsalted butter**

½ cup packed **dark brown sugar**

1 (14-ounce) can **sweetened condensed milk**

½ teaspoon **kosher salt**

1 very ripe medium **banana**, finely chopped

Vegetable oil, for frying

GLAZE

2 cups **confectioners' sugar**, sifted

1 teaspoon **vanilla extract**

3 tablespoons **whole milk**

1 cup coarsely crushed **graham crackers** or **British digestive biscuits**, such as McVitie's, for topping

1 Make the dough: In a large bowl, stir together 1 teaspoon of the granulated sugar and the yeast. Pour in the warm milk and whisk to combine. Let the yeast mixture stand until foamy, about 10 minutes.

2 Meanwhile, in a medium bowl, whisk together the remaining ¼ cup granulated sugar, the bananas, melted butter, salt, vanilla, and eggs until smooth. Pour the banana mixture into the bowl with the yeast mixture and stir to combine. Add the flour and stir with a wooden spoon until the dough comes together.

3 On a lightly floured work surface, knead the dough until smooth and elastic, 8 to 10 minutes. (If you have a stand mixer, place the dough in the mixer bowl, attach the

(recipe continues)

dough hook to the mixer, and knead the dough on medium speed for 6 to 8 minutes.) Lightly grease a large bowl with butter. Form the dough into a ball, place it in the bowl, and cover with plastic wrap. Let stand in a draft-free area until doubled in size, about 1 hour.

4 Meanwhile, make the filling: Melt the butter in a medium skillet over medium heat. Add the brown sugar and stir until it is incorporated. Add the condensed milk and salt and cook, stirring continuously, until the sugar has been incorporated and the mixture comes to a boil and thickens slightly, about 2 minutes. Remove the skillet from the heat and let the sauce cool completely to room temperature, at least 1 hour.

5 Meanwhile, on a lightly floured work surface, roll the dough until ½ inch thick. Use a 2½- to 3-inch round cutter to cut out 12 rounds of dough, rerolling the scraps, if necessary. Place the dough rounds on the work surface and cover loosely with plastic wrap. Let stand until they puff slightly, about 20 minutes.

6 Fill a large Dutch oven or heavy saucepan with vegetable oil to a depth of 2 inches. Attach a deep-fry thermometer to the side and heat the oil over medium-high heat to 350°F. Line a baking sheet with paper towels and set it nearby.

7 While the oil heats, make the glaze: In a small bowl, whisk together the confectioners' sugar, vanilla, and milk until smooth.

8 Using a metal spatula, carefully lift 3 dough rounds and lower them into the hot oil. Fry until golden brown and cooked through, 3 to 4 minutes, turning them once halfway through the cooking time. Using a spider or slotted spoon, transfer the doughnuts to the prepared baking sheet to drain briefly, then transfer them to a wire rack to cool. Repeat frying the remaining doughnuts.

9 When the doughnuts are cool enough to handle, fill them: Stir the chopped banana into the cooled caramel sauce, then transfer the filling to a piping bag fitted with a ½-inch round tip.

10 Using the end of a wooden spoon, pierce the side of each doughnut to the center to create an opening for the piping bag tip. Place the tip in the opening and fill each doughnut with the banana-caramel filling.

11 Dip the top of each doughnut in the glaze, letting the excess run off, then return it to the wire rack. While the glaze is still wet, sprinkle each doughnut with some of the crushed graham crackers. Let the doughnuts stand for 10 minutes more to allow the glaze to set before serving.

CARAMEL APPLE

SKILLET CAKE

This upside-down cake is the kind of dessert you make when you're in a log cabin, sipping hot cider and wearing plaid (or when you want to feel like you are). It's the best parts of a caramel apple—saucy, sweet, and fruity—perched atop a tender cake. Channel your most obsessive qualities when you fan out the apple slices on the caramel sauce: They might get covered up with batter when they go into the oven, but once you flip out the finished cake, they're the stars.

Nonstick cooking spray

¾ cup **all-purpose flour**, plus more for dusting

⅓ cup **granulated sugar**

1 teaspoon **baking powder**

½ teaspoon **kosher salt**

⅓ cup **vegetable oil**

⅓ cup **whole milk**

1 teaspoon **vanilla extract**

2 large **eggs**

1 cup **caramel sauce**, homemade (see page 176, step 4) or store-bought

1 tart **green apple**, such as Granny Smith, peeled, cored, and cut into ¼-inch-thick slices

Vanilla ice cream, for serving

1 Preheat the oven to 350°F. Grease a 9-inch round cake pan with cooking spray, line the bottom with a round of parchment paper cut to fit, and grease the parchment. Dust the pan with flour to coat and tap out any excess.

2 In a large bowl, whisk together the flour, granulated sugar, baking powder, and salt. In a medium bowl, whisk together the vegetable oil, milk, vanilla, and eggs. Pour the oil mixture over the flour mixture and whisk until just combined.

3 Pour the caramel sauce into the prepared pan, then arrange the apple slices in a circular pattern over the bottom of the pan, with each one overlapping the other, until the entire bottom is covered. Pour the cake batter over the apples and smooth out the top with a rubber spatula.

4 Bake the cake until golden brown and a toothpick inserted into the center comes out clean, about 25 minutes. Transfer the pan to a wire rack and let the cake cool in the pan for 20 minutes.

5 Place a large round plate on top of the cake pan, then invert them together. Remove the pan and the parchment paper round. Slice the cake while warm and serve with vanilla ice cream.

CHECKERBOARD CAKE

Even the most mind-racking riddles will make you facepalm when you understand the trick behind them. And the same is true for this cake. With its alternating squares of yellow and chocolate cake, it seems impossibly hard to pull off. But once you know that the geometric design comes from stacking alternating bull's-eyes of yellow and chocolate cake . . . well, you know. (Don't worry: You never have to reveal the riddle's answer to your flabbergasted friends.) Even if you don't want to go through the trouble of checkerboarding (it's worth it!), you'll want to bookmark the recipes for the cakes and the fluffy, eat-it-by-the-spoon chocolate frosting anyway: They're birthday classics.

Nonstick cooking spray

All-purpose flour, for dusting

CHOCOLATE CAKE

1 cup all-purpose flour

⅓ cup unsweetened Dutch-processed cocoa powder

1 teaspoon baking powder

½ teaspoon kosher salt

1 cup granulated sugar

½ cup (1 stick) unsalted butter, at room temperature

1 teaspoon vanilla extract

2 large eggs

½ cup plus 2 tablespoons whole milk

YELLOW CAKE

1½ cups all-purpose flour

1½ teaspoons baking powder

½ teaspoon kosher salt

1 cup granulated sugar

½ cup (1 stick) unsalted butter, at room temperature

1 teaspoon vanilla extract

3 large eggs

½ cup whole milk

CHOCOLATE FROSTING

12 cups confectioners' sugar, sifted

¾ cup unsweetened Dutch-processed cocoa powder

1 teaspoon kosher salt

1½ cups (3 sticks) unsalted butter, at room temperature

1¼ cup heavy cream

2 teaspoons vanilla extract

1 Preheat the oven to 350°F. Grease two 9-inch round baking pans with cooking spray, line the bottoms with rounds of parchment paper cut to fit, and grease the parchment. Dust the pans with flour to coat and tap out any excess.

2 Make the chocolate cake: In a large bowl, whisk together the flour, cocoa powder, baking powder, and salt.

3 Combine the granulated sugar, butter, and vanilla in a separate large bowl. Using a handheld mixer, beat on medium speed until

pale and fluffy, about 3 minutes. Add the eggs one at a time, beating well after each, then beat until smooth. Add the flour mixture in three additions, alternating with the milk, in two additions. Mix until the batter comes together and is smooth.

4 Scrape the batter into one of the prepared pans and smooth out the top with a rubber spatula. Bake the cake until a toothpick inserted into the center comes out clean, 30 to 35 minutes. Transfer the pan to a wire rack and let the cake cool in the pan for 10 minutes (keep the oven on). Invert the cake onto the rack, remove the pan and parchment paper, and let cool completely, about 1 hour.

5 Make the yellow cake: In a large bowl, whisk together the flour, baking powder, and salt.

6 Combine the granulated sugar, butter, and vanilla in a separate large bowl. Using a handheld mixer, beat on medium speed until pale and fluffy, about 3 minutes. Add the eggs one at a time, beating well after each, then beat until smooth. Add the flour mixture in three additions, alternating with the milk, in two additions. Mix until the batter comes together and is smooth.

7 Scrape the batter in the second prepared pan and smooth out the top with a rubber spatula. Bake until the cake is golden brown and a toothpick inserted into the center comes out clean, 30 to 35 minutes. Transfer the pan to a wire rack and let the cake cool in the pan for 10 minutes. Invert the cake onto the rack, remove the pan and parchment paper, and let cool completely, about 1 hour.

8 Make the chocolate frosting: Whisk together the confectioners' sugar, cocoa powder, and salt in a large bowl. Add the butter and, using a handheld mixer, beat on low speed until the sugar has been incorporated and the frosting is very thick. Add the cream and vanilla and beat on low speed, gradually increasing to medium-high, until fluffy and spreadable.

9 Assemble the cake: Slice the tops off both cakes to level them, then halve each cake horizontally to create 4 layers total. (Save or discard the scraps.) Cut out a 6-inch circle from the center of each cake layer, leaving it in place **A** . Cut out a 3-inch circle from the center of each 6-inch circle **B** .

10 Place an outside (9-inch) chocolate cake ring on a plate or cake stand. Insert a middle (6-inch) yellow cake ring, then an inner (3-inch) chocolate cake ring. Frost the cake with 1 cup of the chocolate frosting **C** . Place an outside (9-inch) yellow cake ring over the frosting. Insert a middle (6-inch) chocolate cake ring, then an inner (3-inch) yellow cake ring. Frost the cake with 1 cup of the frosting. Repeat twice more with the remaining cake rings, alternating the colors on the outside and spreading another 1 cup of the frosting between the layers. Frost the top and side of the cake with the remaining frosting **D** .

11 Refrigerate to firm the frosting, at least 1 hour or up to 1 day. Let the cake sit at room temperature for 30 minutes before serving.

tasty dessert

RED RASPBERRY VELVET CUPCAKES

WITH MARBLED CREAM CHEESE FROSTING

Despite its firetruck color, red velvet cake tastes like cocoa. And since raspberries are the perfect partner to chocolate *and* they just so happen to be red, it's only logical to combine the two, right? We're harnessing the natural color of raspberry puree and mixing it into chocolatey red velvet cake batter. (If you want a red that's closer to neon red, you can still add a couple tablespoons of red food coloring, of course.) And, lest we forget the best part, the tangy cream cheese frosting is here, too, only it's swirled with more raspberry puree for a little hint of what lies below.

CUPCAKES

2½ cups **all-purpose flour**

1 tablespoon **unsweetened natural cocoa powder**

1 teaspoon **baking soda**

1 teaspoon **kosher salt**

2 (6-ounce) containers **raspberries**, plus more for garnish, if desired

1½ cups **granulated sugar**

1 cup **buttermilk**, at room temperature

¾ cup **vegetable oil**, plus more if needed

2 tablespoons **liquid red food coloring** (optional)

2 teaspoons **vanilla extract**

1 teaspoon **distilled white vinegar**

2 large **eggs**

FROSTING

2 (8-ounce) packages **cream cheese**, at room temperature

1 cup (2 sticks) **unsalted butter**, at room temperature

1 teaspoon **vanilla extract**

½ teaspoon **kosher salt**

3 cups **confectioners' sugar**

1 Preheat the oven to 350°F. Line 18 muffin tin cups with paper liners.

2 Make the cupcakes: In a large bowl, whisk together the flour, cocoa powder, baking soda, and salt until evenly combined.

3 In a small food processor or blender, puree the raspberries. Scrape the raspberry puree through a fine-mesh strainer into a bowl, pushing it through with a rubber spatula, to remove the seeds. Set aside ¼ cup of the raspberry puree in a small bowl for the frosting. Pour the rest of the raspberry puree into a separate large bowl and whisk in the granulated sugar, buttermilk, vegetable oil, food coloring (if using), vanilla, vinegar, and eggs until smooth.

4 Pour the buttermilk mixture over the flour mixture and stir with a whisk until the batter just comes together. Divide the batter among the prepared muffin cups.

5 Bake until a toothpick inserted into the center of each cupcake comes out clean, 20 to 25 minutes. Transfer the muffin tins to wire racks and let the cupcakes cool in the pans for 20 minutes, then remove the cupcakes from the tins and place them directly on the racks to cool completely, about 1 hour.

6 Make the frosting: Combine the cream cheese, butter, vanilla, and salt in a large bowl. Using a handheld mixer, beat on medium speed until smooth. Sift the confectioners' sugar through a fine-mesh sieve over the cream cheese mixture, then beat on low speed until combined. Increase the speed to medium and beat until lightened and fluffy, about 1 minute. Scrape the reserved ¼ cup raspberry puree into the frosting and use a rubber spatula to fold the puree into the frosting just enough to swirl it, about 5 turns.

7 Transfer the frosting to a piping bag fitted with a 1-inch plain round tip or to a zip-top plastic bag with one corner cut off. Pipe the frosting onto each cupcake. (Alternatively, simply dollop the frosting on each cupcake and spread evenly with a table knife.) Top each cupcake with a whole raspberry, if you like, to garnish.

CONFETTI BIRTHDAY SOUFFLÉ

Just because you think you've "outgrown" birthday cake (and, child, please) doesn't mean you can't get in on the birthday cake festivity (you haven't outgrown fun, too, have you?). Take all of the best parts of a classic birthday cake—rainbow sprinkles and "imitation" vanilla extract (for that authentic boxed cake flavor)—and wrap them into one of the most dramatic, high-stakes desserts out there: a poofy, dramatic soufflé. Since you're upgrading from cake to soufflé, might as well jump from milk to champagne while you're at it.

4 tablespoons (½ stick) **unsalted butter**, plus more for greasing

½ cup **granulated sugar**, plus more for dusting

⅓ cup **all-purpose flour**

9 large **eggs**, separated

1½ cups **whole milk**

2 tablespoons **vanilla extract**, preferably "imitation"

½ cup **rainbow sprinkles**, plus more for garnish

Confectioners' sugar, for garnish

Whipped cream, for serving

1 Preheat the oven to 400°F. Grease a 10-cup (2½-quart) soufflé dish with butter, then dust it with granulated sugar to coat and tap out any excess.

2 In a medium saucepan, whisk together ¼ cup granulated sugar and the flour until combined, then stir in the egg yolks until the mixture forms a thick paste. Pour in the milk and whisk until smooth. Set the pan over medium heat and cook, stirring often with a wooden spoon, until the custard has thickened and coats the back of the spoon, 4 to 6 minutes. Pour the custard through a fine-mesh strainer into a large bowl, pressing it through with a rubber spatula, then stir in

the butter and vanilla until the butter has melted and the custard is smooth. Refrigerate the custard until cool to the touch, at least 30 minutes or up to 1 day.

3 Place the egg whites in a large bowl. Using a handheld mixer, beat on medium speed until foamy and starting to form soft peaks. With the mixer running, pour in the remaining ¼ cup sugar and beat until stiff peaks form.

4 Add one-third of the beaten whites to the chilled custard and stir vigorously until smooth. Add the remaining whites and the sprinkles and use a large rubber spatula to gently fold them in until the batter is smooth. Pour the batter into the prepared soufflé dish and smooth the top. Immediately place in the oven, reduce the oven temperature to 375°F, and bake until risen and golden brown, 35 to 40 minutes.

5 Immediately transfer the soufflé to the table and dust the top with confectioners' sugar. Shower with more sprinkles and serve while hot, spooned onto plates and dolloped with whipped cream.

GUAVA AND CREAM

VICTORIA SPONGE CAKE

Fans of *The Great British Bake Off* won't need an explanation of Victoria sponge. But we'll catch the rest of you up: It's a traditional English tea-time treat that consists of thick layers of jam and whipped cream sandwiched between two tender sponge cakes. We jumped across the pond and gave it a Latin American twist, swapping out the raspberry jam for tropical guava jelly and the whipped cream for tangy, fluffy cream cheese frosting. (If this were a clothing collab, we'd call it "Guava Pastelito by Victoria Sponge.") Serve slices with cups of tea, and even Mary Berry would surely approve.

¾ cup (1½ sticks) **unsalted butter**, at room temperature, plus more for greasing

1½ cups **cake flour**, plus more for dusting

1½ teaspoons **baking powder**

¾ teaspoon **kosher salt**

¾ cup **granulated sugar**

3 large **eggs**

1 (8-ounce) package **cream cheese**, at room temperature

½ cup **confectioners' sugar**

½ teaspoon **vanilla extract**

4 ounces **guava paste**, coarsely chopped

¼ cup **guava jelly**

1   Preheat the oven to 350°F. Grease two 8-inch round cake pans with butter, line the bottoms of each with a round of parchment paper cut to fit, and grease the parchment. Dust the pans with flour to coat and tap out any excess.

2   In a medium bowl, whisk together the flour, baking powder, and ½ teaspoon of the salt.

3   Combine the butter and granulated sugar in a large bowl. Using a handheld mixer, beat on medium-high speed until pale and fluffy, about 5 minutes. Add the eggs one at a time, beating until incorporated after each addition. Add the flour mixture and beat on low speed until the batter just comes together.

4   Divide the batter between the prepared pans and smooth the tops with a rubber spatula. Bake until a toothpick inserted into each comes out clean, 35 to 40 minutes. Transfer to a wire rack and let the cakes cool in the pans for 20 minutes. Invert the cakes onto the rack, remove the pans and paper, then flip the cakes right-side up and let cool completely, about 1 hour.

5   While the cakes cool, combine the cream cheese, confectioners' sugar, vanilla, and remaining ¼ teaspoon salt in a large bowl. Using a handheld mixer, beat on medium speed until smooth and fluffy, 3 to 4 minutes.

6   In a large glass bowl, combine the guava paste and jelly and microwave on high for about 30 seconds, until just warmed through and soft. Using a fork, mash the paste into the jelly until evenly combined.

7   Trim the top of one cake so it's level and place it on a serving plate. Spoon the guava mixture onto the cake in an even layer, leaving a ½-inch border. Flip the second cake over on the rack, rounded-side down, and spread the cream cheese mixture over the bottom, leaving a ½-inch border. Set the second cake over the first so the guava and cream cheese layers are sandwiched. Press the cakes lightly so the fillings come just to the edge. Dust the top with confectioners' sugar and cut into wedges to serve.

CANNOLI ANGEL FOOD
SHEET CAKE

We'll let you in on a little secret: The lowest-maintenance layer cake is not made in round cake pans, but actually on a rimmed baking sheet. Instead of trimming and stacking rounds, you just slice the rectangular cake into two smaller rectangles and place one on top of the other, easy-peasy. Here, we're making that cake a light and spongy angel food so that it can withstand (and take in!) all of the flavors of the silky, cannoli-inspired frosting. And once you taste it—rich from ricotta and flavored with orange zest and pistachios—you'll understand why (and you'll want to eat it with a spoon). To hit the point home, the cake is covered in mini chocolate chips (a crucial cannoli detail!), then topped just before serving with crumbled sugar cones to remind you of that crispy-as-all-get-out pastry shell.

CAKE

Nonstick cooking spray

1½ cups **cake flour**, plus more for dusting

2 cups **egg whites**

1 teaspoon **cream of tartar**

¾ teaspoon **kosher salt**

2 cups **granulated sugar**

½ teaspoon ground **cinnamon**

1 tablespoon **vanilla extract**

FROSTING

1⅓ cups **ricotta cheese** (12 ounces), at room temperature

1 (8-ounce) package **cream cheese**, at room temperature

2 cups **confectioners' sugar**, sifted

2 teaspoons **vanilla extract**

Finely grated zest of 1 **orange**

½ cup finely chopped **pistachios**

½ cup mini **bittersweet** or **semisweet chocolate chips**

½ cup coarsely crushed **sugar ice cream cones**

1 Preheat the oven to 350°F. Coat an 18 by 13-inch rimmed baking sheet with cooking spray, line the bottom with parchment paper, and coat the parchment with cooking spray. Dust the pan with flour to coat completely and tap out any excess.

2 Make the cake: Combine the egg whites, cream of tartar, and salt in a large bowl. Using a handheld mixer, beat on medium-high speed until the egg whites are foamy and start to form soft peaks, about 6 minutes. With the mixer running, slowly pour or spoon in the granulated sugar and cinnamon. Add the vanilla and beat until the whites are glossy, smooth, and form stiff peaks, about 8 minutes.

3 Sift the cake flour through a fine-mesh strainer over the whites, then use a large rubber spatula to fold the flour completely into the whites, until no dry patches remain. Scrape the batter into the prepared baking sheet and smooth the top with the rubber spatula.

(recipe continues)

4 Bake until the cake is golden brown and a toothpick inserted into the center comes out clean, about 20 minutes. Transfer the pan to a wire rack and let the cake cool completely on the pan, about 1 hour.

5 Make the frosting: In a food processor, combine the ricotta, cream cheese, confectioners' sugar, vanilla, and orange zest and process until super smooth.

6 Carefully invert the cake onto a cutting board and remove the parchment paper. Cut the cake in half crosswise and flip each half over so it's right-side up again. Spread half the frosting evenly over one cake half, sprinkle with the pistachios, then stack the other cake half on top. Spread the remaining frosting over the top of the cake all the way to the edges. Sprinkle the top with the chocolate chips. Refrigerate the cake until the frosting is firm, 1 to 2 hours.

7 Let the cake sit at room temperature for 20 minutes. Before serving, sprinkle the top of the cake with the crushed sugar cones, then slice to serve.

DRIPPY & OOZY

basic custard sauce
plus some tasty transformations

makes 3 cups

Think of custard as the shape-shifting superhero of the pastry world. With a little cream and a bit of churning, it's ice cream; with a spoonful of cornstarch, it's pudding; tucked into a pastry shell and topped with berries, it's dessert fit for high tea. And it's delicious by the spoonful, without any additions at all. The trickiest part of this building-blocks sauce—which is made from sugar, eggs, and milk—is cooking it to the right temperature. Luckily, an instant-read thermometer will take away all of the guesswork.

¾ cup **granulated sugar**

½ teaspoon **kosher salt**

6 large **egg yolks**

2 cups **whole milk**

2 teaspoons **vanilla extract**

1 In a medium saucepan, combine the sugar, salt, and egg yolks and stir with a whisk until the mixture forms a thick paste. Stir in the milk until smooth. Set the saucepan over medium heat, and cook, stirring steadily but slowly with a rubber spatula or wooden spoon, until the custard sauce thickens enough to coat the back of the spoon and an instant-read thermometer inserted into the custard reads between 170° and 175°F, 8 to 10 minutes.

2 Remove the pan from the heat and stir in the vanilla. Pour the custard through a fine-mesh strainer into a large bowl. Let the sauce cool to room temperature, stirring occasionally, about 20 minutes.

3 Pour the sauce into a storage container and press a piece of plastic wrap directly against the surface to prevent a skin from forming. Refrigerate until chilled and set (it will have the consistency of loose pancake batter), at least 1 hour or up to 1 week.

TASTY TRANFORMATIONS

① Mix with 1 cup heavy cream and the seeds of 1 vanilla bean, if you like, and churn in an ice cream maker for vanilla bean ice cream.

② Stir ¼ cup all-purpose flour into the sugar-egg mixture and cook as directed to make pastry cream for filling fruit tarts.

③ Stir 2 tablespoons cornstarch into the sugar-egg mixture and cook as directed to make vanilla pudding.

④ Pour over fresh summer berries and top with whipped cream in the summer, or pour over warm fruit cobblers and crisps in the winter.

⑤ Pour over 7 cups chopped stale bread in a 9-inch square pan. Bake at 350°F for 35 to 40 minutes for bread pudding.

⑥ Serve in a bowl with shortbread or other crunchy cookies on the side for dipping.

NO-BAKE 16-LAYER
S'MORES CAKE

You're craving s'mores but you don't have a firepit and you need to feed a crowd. Hey, we've been there, too. This no-bake icebox cake has it all, without the open flame: We've got the graham crackers, the chocolate, and—because we're not monsters—the gooey marshmallows, too. The loaf has to set in the fridge overnight so that the cookies can meld with the other ingredients, but don't worry: The warm ooziness you crave comes at the final moment, when even more warm Fluff is spread over the finished cake and oozes down the sides, just like the marshmallow over the fire.

2½ cups **semisweet chocolate chips**

2 cups **heavy cream**

3 cups **Marshmallow Fluff**

3 tablespoons **whole milk**

18 to 22 **graham crackers**

2 ounces **bittersweet chocolate**, thinly shaved

1 Place the chocolate chips in a large heatproof bowl. In a small saucepan, bring the heavy cream to a boil over medium-high heat. Pour the cream over the chocolate in the bowl and let stand for 1 minute, undisturbed, then whisk the chocolate and cream together until the chocolate has melted completely and the mixture is thick and smooth.

2 Place 1 cup of the Marshmallow Fluff in a small heatproof bowl and add 1 tablespoon of the milk. Place the remaining 2 cups Fluff in a medium heatproof bowl and add the remaining 2 tablespoons milk. Microwave each bowl of Fluff on high power for 15 seconds to loosen slightly, then stir to incorporate the milk. Cover the smaller bowl of Fluff and refrigerate until ready to serve the cake.

3 Line the bottom and two long sides of a 9 by 5-inch loaf pan with parchment paper and place a row of graham crackers over the bottom of the pan, breaking them as necessary to fit. Pour a thin layer of the Marshmallow Fluff, about 2 tablespoons, over the graham crackers and use a spoon or small rubber spatula to spread it evenly. Place another row of graham crackers on top of the Fluff, then pour a thin layer of the chocolate ganache, about 2 tablespoons, over the crackers and use a spoon or small rubber spatula to spread it evenly. Repeat this layering three more times. Reserve any remaining graham crackers. Cover the loaf pan with plastic wrap and refrigerate overnight to set.

4 Remove the cake and reserved small bowl of Fluff from the refrigerator. Using the parchment paper as handles, lift the cake out of the pan, set it on a serving plate, and discard the parchment. Microwave the Fluff on high power for 15 seconds to loosen, then scrape it onto the cake, letting it drip over the sides. (If desired, use a small kitchen torch to toast the Marshmallow Fluff all over the cake.) Sprinkle with the shaved chocolate and cut into thin slices to serve.

STICKY BUN CAKE

The best thing since sliced bread? Using that sliced bread as the "dough" for a crowd-sized cinnamon roll that has cream cheese filling and a sticky caramel glaze on the top, on the bottom, and dripping down the sides. You don't have to wait for yeast to proof or dough to rise, so these rolls can be ready when you want them.

Nonstick cooking spray

All-purpose flour, for dusting

3 (8-ounce) packages cream cheese, at room temperature

½ cup confectioners' sugar

½ cup whole milk

2 teaspoons vanilla extract

1½ cups (3 sticks) unsalted butter

1 cup packed light brown sugar

¼ cup honey

1 teaspoon kosher salt

1 cup whole pecans

30 slices white bread, crusts removed

1 tablespoon granulated sugar

2 teaspoons ground cinnamon

1 Preheat the oven to 325°F. Coat an 8-inch-wide, 3-inch-tall round cake pan with cooking spray, line the bottom with parchment paper cut to fit, and coat the parchment with cooking spray. Dust the pan with flour.

2 Combine the cream cheese, confectioners' sugar, milk, and 1 teaspoon of the vanilla in a large bowl. Using a handheld mixer, beat on medium-low speed until smooth, about 1 minute. Refrigerate until ready to use, at least 1 hour and up to 1 day.

3 In a saucepan, combine ¾ cup (1½ sticks) butter, the brown sugar, honey, salt, and 1 teaspoon vanilla. Heat over medium heat, stirring, until the sauce is smooth and just comes to a simmer. Pour ¾ cup of the caramel sauce into the bottom of the prepared pan and sprinkle it evenly with the pecans. Reserve the remaining sauce.

4 Arrange 5 slices of bread end to end so they overlap by ½ inch. Press the edges together to adhere them to each other A . Repeat with the remaining bread to make 6 strips total, using 5 slices for each.

5 Place the remaining 1½ sticks of the butter in a small heatproof bowl and microwave on high power until melted. Stir in the granulated sugar and cinnamon until smooth. Using a pastry brush, brush the cinnamon-butter mixture evenly over all 6 bread strips B , then spread the chilled cream cheese filling evenly over the bread strips as well C .

6 Roll up one of the bread strips like a cinnamon roll D , then roll another strip around it to make a bigger roll. Continue until all the strips have been used. If the roll gets too big to maneuver, lay it on its side and wrap the bread strips around it. Place the roll inside the prepared pan on top of the caramel and pecans. Pour the remaining caramel over the roll E and spread it evenly with a rubber spatula F .

7 Bake until the top is bubbling and crisp, about 40 minutes. Transfer to a wire rack and let the roll cool in the pan for 10 minutes.

8 Place a large plate over the top of the cake pan and, using oven mitts, invert the roll onto the plate. Remove the pan and parchment paper and let the roll cool for 10 minutes more to set. Slice while warm and serve.

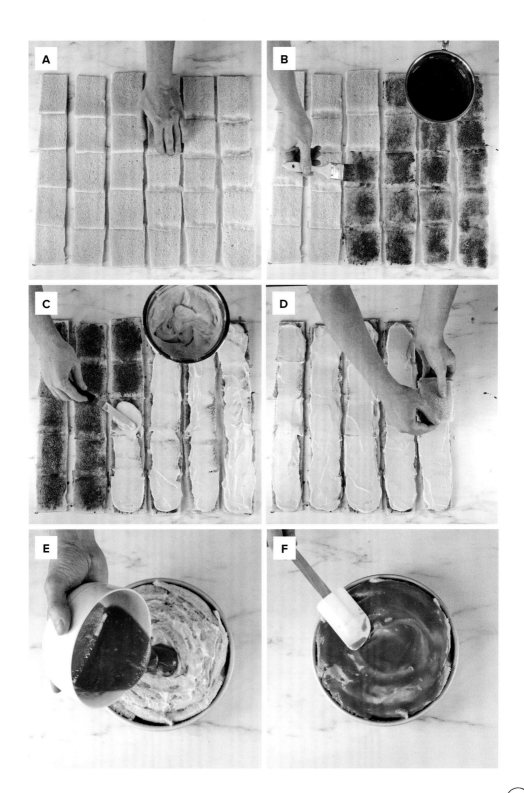

INVISIBLE APPLE CAKE

serves 8

WITH CARAMEL AND ALMONDS

This loaf is more apple than cake (hence the name "invisible") and, if you do it right, more caramel sauce than apple (hence its glorious deliciousness). Drizzle each warm slice—a mosaic of barely held-together apples crowned with toasty almonds—with a generous helping of the buttery sauce and a spoonful of whipped cream for a dessert experience that's somewhere between caramel apple and apple fritter.

CAKE

Nonstick cooking spray

⅔ cup **all-purpose flour**, plus more for dusting

⅓ cup **granulated sugar**

1 teaspoon **kosher salt**

2 large **eggs**

¼ cup plus 3 tablespoons **whole milk**

1½ tablespoons **unsalted butter**, melted

2 sweet-tart **apples**, such as Fuji or Pink Lady, peeled, cored, and cut into ⅛-inch-thick slices

¼ cup sliced **almonds**

CARAMEL SAUCE

⅔ cup **granulated sugar**

3 tablespoons **unsalted butter**

1 cup **heavy cream**, at room temperature

Whipped cream, for serving

1   Preheat the oven to 350°F. Coat an 8 ½ by 4½-inch loaf pan with cooking spray, line the bottom and two long sides with a sheet of parchment paper, and coat the parchment with cooking spray. Dust the pan with flour to coat and tap out any excess.

2   Make the cake: In a medium bowl, vigorously whisk together the sugar, salt, and eggs until pale and lightened, about 1 minute. Stir in the milk and melted butter until smooth. Add the flour and whisk to combine (there will be some lumps). Add the sliced apples and stir with a spoon to coat the apples with the batter.

3   Pour the apples and batter into the prepared pan, then sprinkle the sliced almonds evenly over the top. Cover with foil and bake for 10 minutes. Remove the foil and bake until the cake is golden brown on top and a toothpick inserted into the center comes out clean, about 40 minutes more. Transfer the pan to a wire rack and let the cake cool in the pan for 20 minutes.

4   Meanwhile, make the caramel sauce: In a small saucepan, heat the sugar over medium heat, swirling the pan occasionally, until the sugar dissolves and turns into an amber-colored caramel. Using a rubber spatula, stir in the butter until melted, then stir in the cream until smooth. Remove the pan from the heat and pour the caramel sauce into a serving bowl to cool.

5   Using the overhanging parchment paper as handles, lift the apple cake out of the pan and set it on a cutting board. Cut into thick slices while warm and serve on a plate, drizzled with some of the caramel sauce and topped with a dollop of whipped cream, if you like.

ORANGE-GLAZED

PULL-APART BREAD

In standard-issue monkey bread, each ball of biscuit dough is coated in butter and cinnamon sugar, then baked in a Bundt pan until you have a golden-brown ring of puffed dough with knobs and nodules begging to be pulled off and devoured. We're taking a shortcut to the finish line with store-bought biscuit dough and brightening things up a bit with plenty of fresh orange zest. We wouldn't—we couldn't!—skip out on the best part: the sweet glaze that gets poured over the top. Normally that's caramel sauce, but ours, in keeping with the theme, is orangey. You can cut wide slices of the finished bread with a serrated knife, of course, but it's more fun to rip it apart with your hands—don't mind the sticky mess on your fingers.

1 cup (2 sticks) **unsalted butter**, melted and cooled, plus more for greasing

2 (16-ounce) cans **refrigerated biscuit dough**

½ cup **granulated sugar**

½ cup packed **light brown sugar**

1 teaspoon **vanilla extract**

½ teaspoon **kosher salt**

Finely grated zest of 2 **oranges**

1½ cups **confectioners' sugar**, sifted

2 to 3 tablespoons fresh **orange juice**

1 Preheat the oven to 325°F. Grease a 10-cup Bundt pan with butter.

2 Cut each biscuit into quarters and place them in a large bowl. Add the melted butter, granulated sugar, brown sugar, vanilla, salt, and orange zest and toss until the biscuit pieces are evenly coated in the butter mixture.

3 Transfer the biscuits and any butter mixture in the bowl to the prepared pan. Bake the monkey bread until golden brown and puffed and a toothpick inserted into the center comes out clean, 50 to 55 minutes.

4 Transfer the pan to a wire rack and let the monkey bread cool in the pan for 10 minutes. Invert the monkey bread onto the rack, remove the pan, and let cool completely.

5 Meanwhile, stir the confectioners' sugar and orange juice together in a small bowl to form a thick glaze.

6 Drizzle the glaze evenly over the cooled monkey bread and let stand for 10 minutes to set the glaze before serving.

MAPLE-WALNUT TUILE
ICE CREAM SANDWICHES

It's not just any cookie that makes the ideal ice cream sandwich. Nope, the cookies should be either soft and chewy, so they bend and flex even when frozen, or thin and snappy, like these maple-flavored tuiles, so they shatter easily, joining with the ice cream below. Because the cookies are delicate and lacy, the ice cream seeps through in every bite. Eat these toward the end of summer, on a day when it's hot enough to lick the drippy ice cream off your wrists yet close enough to autumn to daydream about maple syrup waterfalling down a pancake stack on a chilly morning.

Nonstick cooking spray (optional)

½ cup **maple sugar**

2 tablespoons **granulated sugar**

½ teaspoon **kosher salt**

4 large **egg whites**, lightly beaten

¼ cup finely chopped **walnuts**

4 tablespoons (½ stick) **unsalted butter**, melted and cooled

3 tablespoons **all-purpose flour**

1½ pints **vanilla** or **maple-flavored ice cream**

1   Preheat the oven to 350°F. Line a rimmed baking sheet with a silicone baking mat or a sheet of parchment paper coated with cooking spray.

2   In a large bowl, whisk together the maple sugar, granulated sugar, salt, and egg whites until smooth. Add the walnuts, melted butter, and flour and mix until evenly combined.

3   Drop tablespoons of the batter onto the prepared baking sheet and use the back of the tablespoon to spread the batter into thin rounds, about 4 inches in diameter (you should get 4 rounds on one baking sheet).

4   Bake until the rounds are golden brown at the edges but still light colored in the center, about 10 minutes. Using an offset metal spatula, immediately lift each round off the baking sheet while hot and transfer to a wire rack to cool. Repeat with the remaining batter to make 16 cookies total.

5   Flip half the cookies upside down and top each with a 1½-ounce scoop (or 3 tablespoons) of ice cream. Sandwich with the remaining cookies and immediately transfer to a baking sheet. Freeze to firm the ice cream, at least 1 hour or up to 1 day. Serve frozen.

TRES "NUT LECHES" CAKE
WITH DULCE DE LECHE

serves 8

With three types of milk—evaporated, sweetened condensed, and cream—that flood and fill an airy cake, traditional tres leches is just about the most dairy-packed dessert imaginable. So how the heck did we veganize it? We tagged out the dairy for three types of alt milks (yes, in 2019, you can "milk" an oat!), each of which is flavorful in its own right. It might be a bit untraditional to sidestep the dairy, but we stayed true to the important tres leches texture: The cake should be so soaked with creamy syrup that it can't absorb any more liquid, and so soft that you can spoon into it like pudding.

SYRUP

1 cup **unsweetened vanilla almond milk**, or rice or soy milk

1 cup **rich nut milk**, such as macadamia or cashew

1 cup **unsweetened oat** or **full-fat coconut milk**

1 cup **granulated sugar**

CAKE

Nonstick **coconut oil** cooking spray

1½ cups **all-purpose flour**, plus more for dusting

1½ cups **unsweetened vanilla almond milk**, or rice or soy milk

1½ tablespoons fresh **lemon juice**

¼ cup plus 2 tablespoons **cornstarch**

1 tablespoon **baking powder**

½ teaspoon **baking soda**

1 teaspoon **kosher salt**

1 cup **granulated sugar**

½ cup **vegetable oil**

1 tablespoon **vanilla extract**

DULCE DE LECHE

2 (14-ounce) cans **unsweetened full-fat coconut milk**

1½ cups packed **dark brown sugar**

1 teaspoon **kosher salt**

1 Make the soaking syrup: In a medium saucepan, stir together the almond milk, the rich nut milk, oat or coconut milk, and granulated sugar. Bring to a boil over high heat, stirring continuously, then reduce the heat to medium and cook, stirring occasionally, until the mixture has reduced and thickened enough to coat the back of the spoon, 20 to 25 minutes. Remove the saucepan from the heat and set the soaking syrup aside to cool while you make the cake.

2 Preheat the oven to 350°F. Coat a 10-inch angel food or tube pan with cooking spray, dust the pan with flour to coat, and tap out any excess.

3 Make the cake: In a liquid measuring cup, combine the almond milk and the lemon juice and let stand until "curdled," about 10 minutes.

4 In a large bowl, whisk together the flour, cornstarch, baking powder, baking soda, and salt.

5 In a medium bowl, whisk together the granulated sugar, the "curdled" almond milk, vegetable oil, and vanilla until smooth. Pour the vegetable oil mixture over the flour mixture and whisk until just combined. Pour the batter into the prepared pan and smooth out the top with a rubber spatula.

6   Bake until a toothpick inserted into the
    center of the cake comes out clean, about
    30 minutes. Transfer the pan to a wire rack
    and let the cake cool for 5 minutes. Using
    a long skewer or clean toothpick, poke the
    cake all over, spacing the holes evenly. While
    the cake is still warm, gently and slowly pour
    the soaking syrup over the cake until it has
    completely absorbed the syrup. Let the cake
    cool to room temperature, about 1 hour,
    then refrigerate for at least 4 hours or up to
    overnight.

7   Make the dulce de leche: In a medium
    saucepan, stir together the coconut milk,
    brown sugar, and salt. Bring to a boil over

high heat, stirring continuously, then reduce
the heat to medium and cook, stirring
occasionally, until reduced by half and
thickened to a dark caramel–colored sauce,
30 to 35 minutes. Pour the dulce de leche
into a bowl and let cool to room temperature,
at least 1 hour or up to overnight.

8   Run a knife around the outer edge and inner
    tube of the pan to release the cake. Invert
    a serving plate over the pan, then flip the
    plate and pan together, letting the cake fall
    onto the plate. Cut the cake into wedges and
    serve chilled, with the dulce de leche drizzled
    over the top.

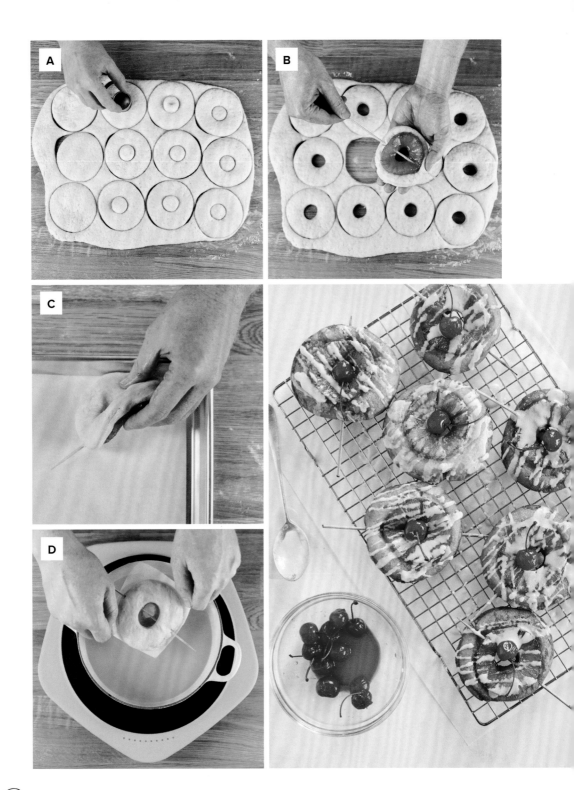

PINEAPPLE UPSIDE-DOWN
DOUGHNUTS

You'll have a hard time convincing your friends that you didn't buy these over-the-top doughnuts from that new place down the street. Seriously, you'll want to take in-process photos as proof. Each airy doughnut is a work of art, a miniature upside-down cake complete with a ring of pineapple, a maraschino cherry, and a sweet glaze. The flavors (yeasty, milky, fruity!) are as interesting as the textures: airy, crispy, and, when you bite into the pineapple, juicy. Don't be scared to drop the parchment paper into the hot oil: As the doughnuts cook, the parchment paper will naturally release, making it easy for you to fish it out.

DOUGH

¼ cup plus 1 teaspoon **granulated sugar**

2 (¼-ounce) packets **active dry yeast**

½ cup warm **water** (105° to 110°F)

¾ cup **whole milk**

⅓ cup **vegetable shortening**, plus more for greasing

1 teaspoon **kosher salt**

2 teaspoons **vanilla extract**

2 large **eggs**, lightly beaten

4 cups **all-purpose flour**, plus more for dusting

TOPPING

4 tablespoons (½ stick) **unsalted butter**

½ cup packed **dark brown sugar**

2 tablespoons **dark rum**

½ teaspoon **kosher salt**

12 canned **pineapple** slices, drained

Vegetable oil, for frying

GLAZE

4 cups **confectioners' sugar**, sifted

¼ cup plus 2 tablespoons **whole milk**

1 teaspoon pure **vanilla extract**

12 **maraschino cherries**, drained

1 Make the dough: In a large bowl, stir together 1 teaspoon of the granulated sugar and the yeast. Pour in the warm water and whisk to combine. Let the yeast mixture stand until foamy, about 10 minutes.

2 Meanwhile, in a small saucepan, combine the milk and shortening and heat over medium heat until the shortening has fully melted. Remove the pan from the heat and stir in the remaining ¼ cup granulated sugar and the salt until dissolved. Let cool slightly. Whisk in the vanilla and eggs until smooth, then pour the milk mixture into the bowl with the yeast mixture and whisk to combine. Add the flour and stir with a wooden spoon until the dough comes together.

3 On a lightly floured work surface, knead the dough until smooth and elastic, 8 to 10 minutes. (If you have a stand mixer, place the dough in the mixer bowl, attach the dough hook to the mixer, and knead the dough on medium speed for 6 to 8 minutes.) Lightly grease a large bowl with shortening. Form the dough into a ball and place it in the bowl. Cover with plastic wrap and let stand in a draft-free area until doubled in size, about 1 hour.

(recipe continues)

4   Meanwhile, make the topping: Line two large baking sheets with parchment paper.

5   Melt 2 tablespoons of the butter in a large nonstick skillet over medium heat. Add ¼ cup of the brown sugar, 1 tablespoon of the rum, and ¼ teaspoon of the salt, and cook, stirring, until the sugar has dissolved and the sauce is smooth. Add 6 pineapple slices to the pan in an even layer and cook, turning occasionally, until the butter starts separating from the sugar and the pineapple rings are well caramelized, about 10 minutes.

6   Remove the skillet from the heat and, using two forks, transfer the pineapple rings to one of the prepared baking sheets, spacing them evenly apart. Rinse the skillet and wipe it dry, then repeat with the remaining butter, brown sugar, rum, salt, and pineapple slices, placing them on the second prepared baking sheet.

7   On a lightly floured work surface, roll out the dough to a 12 by 14-inch rectangle, ½ inch thick. Using a 3½-inch round cutter, cut out 12 rounds of dough, then use a 1-inch round cutter to punch out the center of each round **A** ; save the holes, if you like. Place 1 pineapple ring over a dough circle and weave a long skewer through the edges of the dough ring to attach it to the pineapple ring, making sure the skewer goes through the pineapple ring in two sides and not on top of it **B** . Place the doughnut on the baking sheet, pineapple-side down **C** , and repeat with the remaining dough circles and pineapple rings. Let the doughnuts stand until they puff slightly, about 20 minutes.

8   Fill a large Dutch oven or heavy saucepan with vegetable oil to a depth of 2 inches. Attach a deep-fry thermometer to the side and heat the oil over medium-high heat to 350°F. Line a baking sheet with paper towels and set it nearby.

9   While the oil heats, make the glaze: In a medium heatproof bowl, stir together the confectioners' sugar, milk, and vanilla and microwave on high heat until warm and loosened, 10 to 20 seconds. Stir again until smooth, then set aside and keep warm.

10 Using scissors, carefully cut the parchment around each doughnut. Using the parchment paper as an aide, lower the doughnut into the oil, paper-side down **D** ; repeat with a second doughnut. Fry the doughnuts, removing the parchment as it releases naturally from the doughnuts, until the bottom side is golden brown, about 2 minutes. Using a spider or slotted spoon, carefully flip the doughnuts and fry until golden brown on the second side, about 2 minutes more. Transfer the doughnuts, pineapple-side down, to the prepared baking sheet to drain briefly, then set them pineapple-side up on a wire rack to cool. Repeat to fry the remaining doughnuts, working in batches of two. If you saved the doughnut holes, fry them now until golden brown, 1 to 2 minutes, then drain.

11 While the doughnuts are hot, drizzle the glaze evenly over them, letting the excess drip off, then let cool completely to allow the glaze to set, about 15 minutes. Rest 1 cherry in the center of each. Toss any extra glaze with the doughnut holes until coated.

12 Grabbing a skewer with your fingers, rotate it in place to loosen it first, then pull it out from the doughnut. Repeat with the remaining doughnuts. Serve within 2 hours.

CARAMEL-COCONUT
BREAD PUDDING
WITH CHOCOLATE SAUCE

serves 8

Some bread puddings toe the line between brunch and dessert, but this is not one of them. The bread is layered with caramel sauce and coconut flakes, then soaked in sweet custard so that every cube is creamy soft. And if that weren't enough, once the pudding comes out of the oven, with a top that's puffed and bronzed, each helping is drizzled with warm fudge sauce until it resembles your favorite chocolate-striped cookie. So, yes, it's definitely dessert—but that doesn't mean you'll be able to wait until after dinner to go at it.

½ cup (1 stick) **unsalted butter**, melted and cooled, plus more for greasing

2 cups **whole milk**

1 cup **granulated sugar**

1 teaspoon **vanilla extract**

6 large **eggs**

8 ounces **soft caramel candies**, such as Kraft Caramels (about 27)

⅔ cup **heavy cream**

1 (1-pound) loaf day-old **white country** or **French bread**, cut into 1-inch cubes (about 11 cups)

½ cup **unsweetened flaked coconut**

1½ cups **bittersweet chocolate chips**

1 (14-ounce) can **sweetened condensed milk**

Flaky sea salt

1 Preheat the oven to 350°F. Grease a 9 by 13-inch baking dish with butter.

2 In a large bowl, whisk together the melted butter, milk, sugar, vanilla, and eggs until smooth.

3 In a medium glass bowl, combine the caramels and ⅓ cup cream and microwave on high until melted, about 1½ minutes. Stir the caramel sauce until smooth.

4 Spread half the bread cubes over the bottom of the prepared baking dish, then drizzle the caramel sauce evenly over the bread. Sprinkle half the coconut over the caramel sauce. Top with the remaining bread, then pour the egg mixture evenly over the top. Let stand for 10 minutes to allow the bread time to soak up the egg mixture, then press gently on the bread to ensure the egg mixture is evenly absorbed. Sprinkle the remaining coconut over the top.

5 Bake the bread pudding until golden brown and puffed, 50 to 55 minutes. Transfer the baking dish to a wire rack and let the bread pudding cool for 5 minutes.

6 While the bread pudding cools, in a medium heatproof bowl, stir together the remaining ⅓ cup cream, the chocolate chips, and the condensed milk and microwave on high for 2 minutes, then stir the fudge sauce until smooth.

7 Spoon the bread pudding onto serving plates and drizzle the fudge sauce back and forth over each serving to mimic the stripes of a cookie. Sprinkle with flaky sea salt and serve warm.

TURTLE PROFITEROLES

You'll be glad to know that there are no real turtles involved in the making of these ice cream–stuffed cream puffs. "Turtle," in this instance, refers not to the slow-poke reptiles, but to the old-fashioned candies made from caramel-coated, chocolate-dipped pecans. We've deconstructed those candies (how *Top Chef* of us!) and translated the flavors into profiteroles. It turns out that when you slice an airy cream puff in half, you have two miniature bowls that are perfect for catching ice cream and the chocolate sauce, caramel, and toasted pecans that "turtle" it.

DOUGH

4 tablespoons (½ stick) **unsalted butter**

¼ teaspoon **kosher salt**

⅔ cup **all-purpose flour**

3 large **eggs** (2 left whole, 1 lightly beaten)

SAUCES

½ cup **bittersweet chocolate chips**

1 cup **granulated sugar**

¾ cup **heavy cream**

½ teaspoon **kosher salt**

SERVING

Vanilla or **butter-pecan ice cream**

Chopped toasted **pecans**

1   Preheat the oven to 425°F. Line a large baking sheet with parchment paper.

2   Make the dough: In a medium saucepan, combine the butter, salt, and ½ cup water and bring to a boil over high heat. Add the flour, reduce the heat to medium-low, and cook, stirring continuously with a wooden spoon, until the dough forms a ball and easily pulls away from the side of the pan, about 2 minutes. Remove the pan from the heat and let the dough cool for 5 minutes.

3   Add 1 of the whole eggs and stir with the wooden spoon until completely incorporated, then add the remaining whole egg and stir until incorporated. Pour half the beaten egg into the dough and stir until incorporated and the dough is thick, shiny, and smooth; when you lift the spoon out of the dough, the dough should form a "V" shape.

4   Transfer the warm dough to a large piping bag fitted with a ¾-inch plain round tip. Pipe 1½-inch-wide mounds of the dough onto the prepared baking sheet, spacing them 1 inch apart. In a small bowl, stir together the remaining beaten egg and 1 tablespoon water to make an egg wash, then brush it gently over the dough mounds.

5   Bake until the dough has puffed, about 10 minutes. Without opening the oven, reduce the oven temperature to 350°F and bake the cream puffs until well browned and crisp, about 15 minutes more. Turn the oven off, prop the door open with the handle of a wooden spoon, and let the cream puffs cool completely in the oven, about 1 hour.

6   While the cream puffs cool, make the caramel and fudge sauces: Place the chocolate chips in a small glass bowl. In a medium saucepan, heat the granulated sugar over medium-high heat, stirring often with a rubber spatula or

wooden spoon, until the sugar melts into a dark amber caramel. Pour in the cream (it will bubble up violently), reduce the heat to medium-low, and cook, stirring, until the sauce is smooth. Stir in the salt.

7 Pour ½ cup of the hot caramel sauce over the chocolate chips in the bowl and stir until the chocolate has melted and the mixture is smooth. Pour the remaining caramel sauce into a small bowl.

8 Remove the cream puffs from the oven and, using a serrated knife, split each one open like a hamburger bun. Place small scoops of ice cream into each puff bottom, add the top, and place 3 cream puffs on each serving plate. Drizzle the cream puffs with the caramel sauce and the fudge sauce, then sprinkle them with pecans and serve immediately.

ACKNOWLEDGMENTS

Producers
Kiano Moju
Hector Gomez
Matthew Johnson
Tiffany Lo
Rie McClenny
Nathan Ng
Claire Nolan
Greg Perez
Hitomi Aihara
Adam Bianchi
Jody Tixier
Julie Klink
Cedee Sandoval
Isabel Castillo
Alix Traeger
Andrew Ilnyckyj
Joey Firoben
Crystal Hatch
Ryan Panlasigui
Rachel Gaewski
Kahnita Wilkerson
Betsy Carter
Katie Aubin
Chris Salicrup
Cyrus Kowsari
Diana Lopez
Scott Loitsch
Merle O'Neal
Vaughn Vreeland
Jordan Kenna
Brenda Blanco
Gwenaelle Le
Cochennec
Pierce Abernathy
Alvin Zhou
Marie Telling
Andrew Gauthier
Frank Tiu
Matthew Ciampa
Ashley McCollum
Angela Ruffin
Maira Correa
Tanner Smith
Nick Guillory
Bryanna Duca
Stephen Santayana
Lauren Weitz
Gabi D'Addario
Stevie Ward
Claire King
Alexis deBoschnek
Chloe Morgan
Carrie Hildebrand

Angie Thomas
Dee Robertson
Kate Staben
Mike Goodman
Camille Bergerson
Swasti Shukla
Hannah Williams
Becca Park
Allex Tarr
Jess Maroney
Mike Price
Dylan Keith
Tracy Raetz
Ryan Panlasigui
Grace Lee
Robert Gilstrap
Ken Orlino
Liza Kahn
Katie Schmidbauer
Nora Campbell
Melissa Ng
Sarah Freeark
Leigh Riemer
Brendan Kelly
Jordan Ballantine
Matt Cullum
Ellie Holland
Evelyn Liu
Toby Stubbs
Gaspar Jose
Isadora Manzaro
Suria Rocha
Guta Batalha
Vitor Hugo Tsuru
Agatha Da Hora
Leticia Almeida
Vanessa Hernandez
Lucia Plancarte
Karla Agis
Gus Serrano
Erich Mendoza
Javier Aceves
Thilo Kasper
Dani Beck
Sebastian Fiebrig
Pierre d'Almeida
Pierre Michonneau
Jun Tsuboike
Yui Takahashi
Saki Yamada
Daisuke Furuta
Daiki Nakagawa
Rumi Yamazaki
Ryo Yamaguchi

Sonomi Shimada
Sam Balinghasay
Sara Gulotta
Randy Karels
Swati Vauthrin
Graham Wood
Ryan Inman
Will Kalish
Jeremy Back
Edgar Sanchez
Jess Anastasio
Caitlin Osbahr
Amir Shaikh
Meghan Heintz
Emma Byrne
Shema Kalisa
Sami Simon
Kiyana Salkeld
Paul Marino
Dan Tann
Steve Peterson
Charlyn Buchanan
Jay Henry

Bloggers, chefs, and recipe developers who inspired some of the recipes in this book
- No-Bake 16-Layer S'Mores Cake—My Kaotic Kitchen
- Sticky Bun Cake—Twisted Food
- Hong Kong–Style Egg Custard Tarts—China Sichuan Food
- Dairy-Free Carrot Cake—Loving It Vegan
- Checkerboard Cake—My Cake School
- Super-Soft Banana Bread Cookies—The Girl Who Ate Everything
- Crème Brûlée Cookies—Fine Cooking
- Striped Cookies & Cream Cake—Yotam Ottolenghi
- Peach Cobbler–Stuffed Beignets—The Sits Girls
- Berries and Cream Puff Ring—Joy of Baking

- Soft and Chewy Snickerdoodles—Cake Whiz
- Rocky Road Ice Cream Cake—Kraft Recipes
- Salted Caramel Brownies—Something Swanky
- Chocolate Ripple Cheesecake—Amanda Tastes

Everyone at Clarkson Potter
Amanda Englander
Gabrielle Van Tassel
Stephanie Huntwork
Jan Derevjanik
Marysarah Quinn
Chloe Aryeh
Mark McCauslin
Ivy McFadden
Philip Leung
Merri Ann Morrell
Alexandria Martinez
Linnea Knollmueller
Derek Gullino
Aislinn Belton
Kate Tyler
Carly Gorga
Natasha Martin
Aaron Wehner
Doris Cooper
Jill Flaxman
Katie Ziga
Christine Edwards
John Dawson
David Sanford

Original recipe developer
Ben Mims

Recipe testers
Megan Cornell
Jackie Park

INDEX

To our Tasty family who like (comment
and share) sweets as much as we do!

Published in the United States by
Clarkson Potter/Publishers, an imprint of
the Crown Publishing Group, a division of
Penguin Random House LLC, New York.
crownpublishing.com
clarksonpotter.com

CLARKSON POTTER is a trademark and
POTTER with colophon is a registered
trademark of Penguin Random House LLC.

Library of Congress Cataloging-in-
Publication Data
Names: Tasty, author. Clarkson Potter
  (Firm), publisher.
Title: Tasty dessert: all the sweet you
  can eat.
Description: First edition. | New York :
  Clarkson Potter/Publishers, [2019]
Identifiers: LCCN 2018039379 (print) |
  LCCN 2018039942 (ebook) | ISBN
  9780525575917 (ebook) | ISBN
  9780525575900 (hardcover)
Subjects: LCSH: Baking. | Confectionery.
  | LCGFT: Cookbooks.
Classification: LCC TX763 (ebook) |
  LCC TX763 .T38 2019 (print) | DDC
  641.85/3—dc23
LC record available at https://lccn.loc.
  gov/2018039379

Some recipes originally appeared on
Tasty.co.

ISBN 978-0-525-57590-0
Ebook ISBN 978-0-525-57591-7
Proprietary ISBN 978-0-525-61649-8

Printed in China

Design by Stephanie Huntwork
Cover photographs by Lauren Volo

10 9 8 7 6 5 4 3 2 1

First Edition